Mr. Maugham Speaking:

"No novel is perfect. Of the ten I have chosen there is not one with which you cannot in some particular find fault . . . Nothing is of greater disservice to the reader than the indiscriminate praise that is sometimes bestowed on certain novels commonly accepted as classics.

"A novel is to be read with enjoyment. If it does not give that it is worthless. This being so, every reader is his own best critic, for he alone knows what he enjoys and what he doesn't. There is no obligation to read fiction."

W. Somerset Maugham, acclaimed throughout the world for his novels and plays which have entertained readers since the beginning of the century, is known for his acid irony and brilliant wit.

For those who already know and love the classics, his unique interpretations will present a stimulating challenge. For others who have yet to make their acquaintance, this book will open the door to new excitements and pleasures in the vast and fascinating world of fiction.

W. Somerset Maugham

selects

THE WORLD'S TEN GREATEST NOVELS

Former Title:
GREAT NOVELISTS AND THEIR NOVELS

A Premier Book
FAWCETT PUBLICATIONS, INC., GREENWICH, CONN.
MEMBER OF AMERICAN BOOK PUBLISHERS COUNCIL, INC.

CONTENTS

THE WORLD'S
TEN GREATEST
NOVELS

"THE TEN BEST NOVELS
OF THE WORLD"

I SHOULD LIKE to tell the reader of this book how the essays it contains came to be written. One day, while I was still in the United States, the editor of *Redbook* asked me to make a list of what in my opinion were the ten best novels in the world. I did so, and thought no more about it.

In a brief commentary to accompany this list of books, I wrote, "the wise reader will get the greatest enjoyment out of reading them if he learns the useful art of skipping." Some time later, an American publisher put before me the suggestion of reissuing these ten novels, eliminating from the text of each the portions it is well to leave unread, and with an introduction to each one written by me. The suggestion interested me, and I set to work. Most of these introductions have been published, somewhat abridged, in the *Atlantic Monthly,* and since they appear to have interested readers it has been thought that they might find it convenient to have them collected in a single volume.

One change had to be made in my original list. I had ended it with Marcel Proust's *Remembrance of Things Past,* but for several reasons this was not included in the proposed series. I do not regret this. Proust's novel, the greatest novel of this century, is of immense length, and it would have been impossible, even with drastic cutting, to reduce it to a reasonable size.

Its success has been prodigious, but it is too soon to assess the value posterity will place on it. Proust's fanatical admirers, of whom I am one, can read every word with interest; in a moment of extravagance I wrote once that I would sooner be bored by Proust than amused by any other writer; but I am prepared now to admit that its various parts are of unequal merit. I have a notion that the future will cease to be interested in those long sections of Proust's book which he wrote under the influence of the psychological and philosophical thought current in his day. Some of this has already been recognized to be erroneous. I think then it will be even more evident than it is now that he was a great humorist and that his power to create characters, original, various and lifelike, puts him on an equality with Balzac, Dickens and Tolstoy. It may be that then an abridged version of his immense work will be issued from which will be omitted those parts which time has stripped of their value and only those parts retained which, because they are of the essence of a novel, remain of enduring interest. *Remembrance of Things Past* will still be a very long novel, but it will be a superb one.

My final list of the ten best novels of the world runs as follows:

> Tom Jones
> Pride and Prejudice
> The Red and the Black
> Old Man Goriot
> David Copperfield
> Wuthering Heights
> Madame Bovary
> Moby Dick
> War and Peace
> The Brothers Karamazov

Let me begin by saying, however, that to talk of the ten best novels in the world is to talk nonsense. There are not ten best novels in the world. It may be that there are a hundred, though even of that I am far from sure; if fifty persons, well read and of adequate culture, were to make lists of the hundred best novels in the world, at least two or three hundred, I believe, would be mentioned more than once; but I think that in these fifty lists, supposing they were made by persons of English speech, the ten novels I have chosen would find a place. I say persons of English speech because at least one of the novels on my list, *Moby Dick,* is still comparatively unknown to the educated European public, and I doubt very much whether it is read in German, Spanish or French by any but professed students of English literature. During the eighteenth century English literature was much read in France, but since then, until recently, the French have not taken great interest in anything that was being written beyond their own frontiers; and a French list of the hundred best novels would certainly include works that are, if not unheard of, little read in the English-speaking countries.

Now this great diversity of opinion can be somewhat easily explained. There is a variety of reasons that may make a particular novel so much appeal to a person, even of sound judgment, that he is led to ascribe outstanding merit to it. It may be that he had read it at a time of life or in circumstances when he was particularly liable to be moved by it, or it may be that its theme or its setting has a more than ordinary significance for him owing to his own predilections or personal associations. I can imagine, for instance, that a passionate lover of music might easily place Henry Handel Richardson's *Maurice Guest* among the ten best novels, and a native of the Five Towns, delighted with the fidelity with which Arnold Bennett described their character and their inhabitants, might in his list place *The Old Wives' Tale*. They are both good novels, but I do not think an unbiased judgment would place either of them among the best ten. The nationality of a reader lends to certain books an interest that inclines him to attribute a greater excellence to them than would be generally admitted. I think, to take an example, that any Frenchman of education, making such a list as I have made, would include Madame de Lafayette's *La Princesse De Cleves;* and rightly, for it has outstanding merits. It is the first phychological novel that was ever written; the story is touching and persuasive, the characters are well and subtly drawn, it is written with distinction and it is commendably brief. It deals with a state of society that is well known to every schoolboy in France, its moral atmosphere is familiar to him from his reading of Corneille and Racine, it has the glamour of association with the most splendid period of French history, and it is a worthy contribution to the golden age of French literature. But to the English or American reader the characters may well seem wooden, their behavior unnatural, and their sense of honor, their attention to their personal dignity, a trifle ridiculous. I do not say they are right to think this, but thinking it, they will never class this book among the best ten novels of the world.

But the chief reason for the great diversity of opinion that exists on the respective merits of novels comes, I think, from the fact that the novel is essentially an imperfect form. No novel is perfect. Of the ten I have chosen there is not one with which you cannot in some particular find fault, and that is what I propose to do when I come to write the introduction to each one; for nothing is of greater disservice to the reader than the indiscriminate praise that is sometimes bestowed on certain books that are commonly accepted as classics. He reads and finds that such and such an incident is grossly improbable, such and such a character unreal and such and such a description tedious. If he is of an impatient temper he will cry that the critics who tell him that the novel he is reading is a masterpiece are a set of fools, and if he is of a modest one he will blame himself and think that it is above his head and not for him; but if he is dogged and persistent he will read on conscientiously, but without enjoyment. But a novel is to be read *with* enjoyment. If it does not give that it is worthless. This being so, every reader is his own best critic, for he alone knows what he enjoys and what he doesn't. There is no obligation to read fiction. The critic can be of service in pointing out what, in his opinion (and this is an important qualification), are the merits of a novel that is generally considered great and what are its defects. But the reader must in the first place be warned, to repeat what I have said before, that he must not look for perfection in a novel.

But before I enlarge upon this statement I wish to say something about readers of fiction. The novelist has the right to demand something of them. He has the right to demand that they should possess the small amount of application that is needed to read a book of three or four hundred pages. He has the right to demand that they should have sufficient imagination to be able to envisage the scenes in which the author seeks to interest them and to fill out in their own minds the portraits he has drawn. And finally the novelist has the right to demand from his readers some power of sympathy, for without it they cannot enter into the loves and sorrows, tribulations, dangers, adventures of the persons of a novel. Unless the reader is able to give something of himself he cannot get from a novel the best it has to give.

Now I will specify what, in my opinion, are the qualities that a good novel should have. It should have a widely interesting theme, by which I mean a theme interesting not only to a clique, whether of critics, professors, highbrows, truck drivers or dish washers, but so broadly human that it is interesting to men and women of all sorts. To give an example of what I mean: one might write a novel on the Montessori system which would be of absorbing interest to educationalists, but I cannot persuade myself that it could be anything but an indifferent novel. The story should be coherent and persuasive; it should have a beginning, a middle and an end, and the end should be the natural consequence of the beginning. The episodes should have probability and should not only develop the theme, but grow out of the story. The creatures of the novelist's invention should be observed with individuality, and their actions should proceed from their characters; the reader must never be allowed to say: So and so would never behave like that; on the contrary he should be obliged to say: That's exactly how I should have expected So and so to behave. I think it is all the better if the characters are in themselves interesting.

Flaubert wrote a novel called *The Sentimental Education,* which has a great reputation among many excellent critics, but he chose deliberately for his hero a man so null, so characterless indeed, that it is impossible to care what he does or what happens to him, and in consequence, for all its merits, the book is hard to read. I think I should explain why I say that characters should be observed with individuality; it is too much to expect the novelist to create characters that are quite new; his material is human nature, and although there are all sorts and conditions of men, the sorts are not infinite in number and novels, stories, plays, epics have been written for so many hundreds of years that the chance is small that an author will create an entirely new character. Casting my mind's eye over the whole of fiction, the only absolutely original creation I can think of is Don Quixote, and I should not be surprised to learn that some learned critic had found a remote ancestry for him also. The author is fortunate if he can see his characters through his own individuality, and if his individuality is sufficiently out of the common to give them an illusive air of originality.

And just as behavior should proceed from character,

so should speech. A fashionable woman should talk like a fashionable woman, a street walker like a street walker, a soda jerker like a soda jerker and a lawyer like a lawyer. The dialogue should neither be desultory nor should it be an occasion for the author to air his opinions; it should serve to characterize the speakers and to advance the story. The narrative passages should be vivid, to the point and no longer than is necessary to make the motives of the persons concerned and the situations in which they are placed clear and convincing. The writing should be simple enough for anyone of ordinary education to read it with ease, and the manner should fit the matter as a well-cut shoe fits a shapely foot. Finally a novel should be entertaining. I have put this last, but it is the essential quality, without which no other quality is of any use. No one in his senses reads a novel for instruction or edification. If he wants instruction or edification he is a fool if he does not go to the books written to instruct and edify.

But even if the novel has all these qualities, and that is asking a lot, there is, like a flaw in a precious stone, a faultiness in the form that renders perfection impossible to attain. A short story is a piece of fiction that can be read according to its length in anything between ten minutes and an hour, and it deals with a single, well-defined subject, an incident or a closely related series of incidents, spiritual or material, which is complete. It should be impossible to add to it or to take away from it. Here, I think, perfection can be reached, and I do not think it would be difficult to collect a considerable number of short stories in which this has in fact been done. But a novel is a piece of indefinite length, it may be as long as *War and Peace,* in which a series of incidents are related and a vast number of characters are displayed through a period of time, or as short as *Carmen.* Now, in order to give probability to his story and to make his characters plausible the author has to narrate a number of facts that are relevant to his story, but that are not in themselves interesting. Incidents often require to be separated by a lapse of time, and the author for the balance of his work has to invent as best he can matter that will fill up this lapse. These passages are known as bridges. Some authors have tried to avoid them and have jumped from, as it were, purple patch of incident to purple patch of incident, but I can think of no instance in which this has proved a success. Most novelists resign themselves to crossing them, and they cross them with more or less skill; but it is only too likely that in the process they will be somewhat tedious.

The author is human, and he has his fads and fancies; the looseness of the form, especially as the novel is written in England and Russia, gives him the opportunity to dilate on any subject dear to his heart, and he seldom has the strength of mind or the critical sense to realize that, however interesting it may be to him, unless it is necessary to the working out of his novel it has no place in it. It is besides almost inevitable that the novelist should be susceptible to the fashions of his day, since after all he has an unusual affectibility, and so he is often led to write what, as the fashion passes, loses its attractiveness. Let me give an instance: until the nineteenth century novelists paid little attention to scenery, a word or two was enough to say all they wanted to say about it; but when the romantic school captivated the public fancy it grew modish to write descriptions for their own sake. A man could not go down the street to buy a toothbrush at a drug store without the author telling you what the houses he passed looked like and what articles were for sale in the shops. Dawn and the setting sun, the starry night, the cloudless sky, the rising and the waning moon, the restless sea, the snow-capped mountains, the dark forests—all gave occasion to interminable descriptions. Many were in themselves beautiful; but they were irrelevant. It took writers a long time to discover that a description of scenery, however poetically observed and admirably expressed, was futile unless it was necessary, that is unless it helped the author to get on with his story or told the reader something it behooved him to know about the persons who took part in it. This is an adventitious imperfection in the novel, but there is yet another that seems inherent. Since it is a work of considerable length it must take some time to write, weeks at least, generally months and occasionally even years. It is impossible for the author to continue so long under the spell of his inspiration. I do not like to use this word. It has a certain pretentiousness when it is applied to prose, and I would prefer to leave it to the poets. The poet practices a nobler art than the novelist; but the novelist has this compensation that whereas a poem, unless of the highest quality, is negligible, a novel may have many faults and yet be far from worthless. But for all that, the novelist writes under the influence, if not of inspiration, of something that for want of a better word I must call the unconscious. Perhaps because it is a vague term of somewhat indefinite meaning it expresses well enough that sense an author has that at his best he is an active agent only in so far that he is putting pen to paper, but that really he is an amanuensis; he finds himself writing things he didn't know he knew, happy thoughts come to him from he knows not where and unexpected notions drop in on him like guests at a surprise party. I don't suppose there is anything very mysterious in this: the unexpected notions are doubtless the effects of long past experiences, the happy thoughts arise from some association of ideas, and the things he thought he didn't know were stored away in the recesses of his memory. The unconscious has brought them to the surface, and there they are flowing freely from pen to paper. But the unconscious is wilful and uncertain; it cannot be forced, and no effort of will can excite it to activity; it is like the wind that bloweth whither it listeth and like the rain that falls on the just and the unjust alike. The practiced writer has various methods of coaxing it to come to his help, but sometimes it remains stubborn. Left to himself then, and in so protracted a work as a novel necessarily is, this happens not seldom; left to himself the author can only fall back on dogged industry and his general competence. It will be a miracle if by these means he can hold his reader's attention.

When I consider how many obstacles the novelist has to contend with, how many pitfalls to avoid, I am not surprised that even the greatest novels are not perfect, I am only surprised that they are not more imperfect than they are. It is largely on this account that it is impossible to pick out ten and say they are the best. I could make a list of ten more that in their different ways are as good as those I have chosen: *Anna Karenina, Crime and Punishment, Cousin Bette, The Charterhouse of Parma, Persuasion, Tristram Shandy, Vanity Fair, Middlemarch, The Ambassadors, Gil Blas.* I could give good reasons for choosing those I have and equally good reasons for choosing those I have just mentioned. My choice is arbitrary.

In the past readers seem to have wanted their novels very long, and the author was often hard put to it to provide more matter for the printer than the story he had to tell required. He hit upon one easy way to do this. Into his novel he inserted stories, sometimes long enough to be called novelettes, which had nothing to do with his theme or at best were tacked on to it with little plausibility. No writer did this with greater nonchalance than Cervantes in *Don Quixote*. These interpolations have always been regarded as a blot on an immortal work, and can only be read now with impatience. Contemporary criticism attacked him on this account, and in the second part of his book he eschewed the bad practice, so producing what is generally thought to be impossible, a sequel that was better than its forerunner; but this did not prevent succeeding writers (who doubtless had not read the criticisms) from using so convenient a device to enable them to deliver to the booksellers a quantity of copy sufficient to make a salable volume. In the nineteenth century new methods of publication exposed novelists to new temptations. Monthly magazines that devoted much of their space to what is somewhat depreciatingly known as light literature achieved great success and so provided authors with the opportunity to bring their work before the public in serial form with profit to themselves. At about the same time the publishers found it to their advantage to issue the novels of popular authors in monthly numbers. In both cases the authors contracted to provide a certain amount of material to fill a certain number of pages. The system encouraged them to be leisurely and long-winded. In France, where they were paid by the line, they did not hesitate to write as many lines as they could. They were working men who had to make a living, and even at that they didn't make a handsome one. On one occasion Balzac, having been to Italy and being impressed (as who wouldn't be?) by the pictures he had seen, interrupted the narrative of the novel he was then writing to insert what was nothing less than an article on them. We know from their own admissions how from time to time the authors of these serials, even the best of them, Dickens, Thackeray, Trollope, found it a hateful burden to be obliged to deliver an installment by a given date. No wonder they padded. No wonder they burdened their stories with irrelevant episodes. Once the printers told Dickens that one of his monthly numbers was two sheets, sixteen pages, short, so he had to sit down and grind them out as best he could. He was experienced in this sort of writing, and it is plain enough that had what he put into these sixteen pages been essential to the conduct of that part of his story he would have written them in the first place.

But there is no reason why the reader should have patience with the defects of a novel, whether they are such as are inherent in the form or attributable to the frailty of the novelist, the fashion of the day or the methods of publishing. A sensible person does not read a novel as a task. He reads it as a diversion. He wants to be taken out of himself. He is prepared to interest himself in the characters and is concerned to see how they act in given circumstances and what happens to them; he sympathizes with their troubles and is gladdened by their joys; he puts himself in their place and to an extent lives their lives. Their view of life, their attitude to the great subjects of human speculation, whether stated in words or shown in action, call forth in him a reaction of surprise, of pleasure or of indignation. But he knews instinctively where his interest lies, and he follows it as surely as a hound follows the scent of a fox. But sometimes through the author's failure he loses the scent. Then he flounders about till he finds it again. He skips.

Everybody skips, but to skip without loss is not easy. It may for all I know be a gift of nature, or it may be something that has to be acquired by experience. Dr. Johnson skipped ferociously, and Boswell tells us that "he had a peculiar facility in seizing at once what was valuable in any book, without submitting to the labour of perusing it from beginning to end." But Boswell was doubtless referring to books of information; if it is a burden to read a novel it is better not to read it at all. But unfortunately, owing to the essential imperfection of the form, the deficiencies of the author or the methods of publication, there are few novels which it is possible to read from beginning to end with unfailing interest. Skipping may be a bad habit, but it is one that is forced upon the reader. But when once a reader starts skipping it is hard to stop, and so he may miss much that it would have been to his advantage to read.

Readers in the past seem to have been more patient

than the readers of today. There were few diversions, and they had more time to read novels of a length that seems to us now inordinate. It may be that they were not irritated by the digressions and irrelevances that interrupted the narration. But some of the novels that suffer from these defects are among the greatest that have ever been written. It is deplorable that on this account they should be less and less read.

It is to induce readers to read them that this series has been designed. The attempt has been made to omit from these ten novels everything but what tells the story the author has to tell, exposes his relevant ideas and displays with adequacy the characters he has created. Some students of literature, some professors and critics, will exclaim that it is a shocking thing to mutilate a masterpiece, and that it should be read as the author wrote it. But do they actually do this? I suggest that they skip what is not worth reading, and it may be that they have cultivated the art of skipping to their profit; but most people haven't: it is surely better that they should have their skipping done for them by someone of taste and discrimination. If he has made a good job of it he should be able to give the reader a novel of which he can read every word with enjoyment.

Coleridge said of *Don Quixote* that it is a book to read through once and then only to dip into, by which he may well have meant that parts of it are so tedious, and even absurd, that it is time ill-spent, when you have once discovered this, to read them again. It is a great and important book, and a professed student of literature should doubtless read it once through (I myself have read it from cover to cover three times), yet I cannot but think that the ordinary reader, the reader who reads for delight, would lose nothing if he did not read the dull parts at all. He would surely enjoy all the more the parts in which the narrative is directly concerned with the adventures and conversations, so amusing and so touching, of the gentle knight and his earthy squire. There is another novel, certainly important, but to be called great only with hesitation, Samuel Richardson's *Clarissa,* which is of a length to defeat all but the most obstinate of novel readers. I do not believe I could ever have brought myself to read it if I had not come upon a copy in an abridged form. The abridgment had been so well done that I had no feeling that anything had been lost.

There is nothing reprehensible in cutting. I don't suppose that any play has ever been produced that was not, to its advantage, more or less drastically cut in rehearsal. I know no reason why a novel should not be subjected to the same process. Indeed we know that most publishers have editors whose particular business it is to do just this, and in most cases the book they have thus dealt with is all the better for it. If readers are led to read the great novels in this series when they would not have done so unless what may well be described as a lot of dead wood had been cut away from them, the efforts of the publishers and the editors will have been well worth while. They will lose nothing that is valuable, and because nothing is left in these volumes but what *is* valuable, they will enjoy to the full a very great intellectual pleasure.

LEO TOLSTOY
and
WAR AND PEACE

I THINK BALZAC is the greatest novelist the world has ever known, but I think Tolstoy's *War and Peace* is the greatest novel. No novel with such a wide sweep, dealing with so momentous a period of history and with such a vast array of characters, was ever written before, nor, I surmise, will ever be written again. It has been justly called an epic. I can think of no other work of fiction that could with truth be so described. Strakhov, a friend of Tolstoy's and an able critic, put his opinion into a few energetic sentences: "A complete picture of human life. A complete picture of the Russia of that day. A complete picture of what may be called the history and struggle of peoples. A complete picture of everything in which people find their happiness and greatness, their grief and humiliation. That is *War and Peace*."

Tolstoy was thirty-six when he began to write it, an age at which an author's creative gift is generally at its height, and it was not till six years later that he finished it. The period he chose was that of the Napoleonic wars, and the climax is Napoleon's invasion of Russia, the burning of Moscow and the retreat and destruction of his armies. When Tolstoy started upon his novel it was with the notion of writing a tale of family life among the gentry, and the historical incidents were to serve merely as a background. The persons of the story were to undergo a number of experiences which would profoundly affect them spiritually, but in the end, after much suffering, they would be purified and enjoy a quiet and happy life. It was only in the course of writing that Tolstoy placed more and more emphasis on the titanic struggle between the opposing powers, and from his extensive reading conceived a philosophy of history to which I shall briefly refer later.

There are said to be something like five hundred characters in the book. They are sharply individualized and clearly presented to the reader. This in itself is a great achievement. The interest is not concentrated as in most novels on two or three persons or even on a single group, but on the members of four families belonging to the aristocracy, the Rostovs, the Bolkonskis, the Kuragins and the Bezukhovs. One of the difficulties a novelist has to cope with when his theme requires him to deal with more groups than one is to make the transition from one to another so plausible that the reader accepts it with docility. He finds then that he has been told for the time what he needs to know about one set of persons and is ready to hear how things have been going with others of whom for a while he has heard nothing. On the whole Tolstoy has managed to do this so skilfully that you seem to be following a single thread of narration.

Like writers of fiction in general Tolstoy framed his characters on persons he knew, or knew of; but of course he used them only as models, and by the time his imagination had worked upon them they had become creatures of his own invention. The thriftless Count is said to have been suggested by his grandfather, Nicholas Rostov by his father and the pathetic, charming Princess Mary by his mother. In the two men who may be taken as the heroes of *War and Peace,* Pierre Bezukhov and Prince Andrew, Tolstoy is generally supposed to have had himself in mind; and it is perhaps not fantastic to suggest that, conscious of his own divided personality, in thus creating two contrasted individuals on the one model of himself he sought to clarify and understand his own character. Pierre and Prince Andrew are alike in this, that like Tolstoy himself both seek mental peace, both look for the answer to the mysteries of life and death, and neither finds it; but otherwise they are very dissimilar. Prince Andrew is a gallant, romantic figure, proud of his race and rank, noble-minded, but haughty, dictatorial, intolerant and unreasonable. He is for all his defects a very engaging character. Pierre is much less so. He is kind, sweet-natured, generous, modest, gentle and self-sacrificing; but so weak, so irresolute, so easily hoodwinked, so gullible that you cannot help feeling impatient with him. His desire to do good, and be good, is touching, but was it necessary to make him such a fool? And when, looking for an answer to the riddles that torment him, he becomes a Freemason, Tolstoy has been led into writing some very, very dull chapters.

Both these men are in love with Natasha, Count Rostov's younger daughter, and in her Tolstoy has created the most delightful girl in fiction. Nothing is so difficult as to portray a young girl who is at once charming and interesting. Generally the young girls of fiction are colorless (Amelia in *Vanity Fair*), priggish (Fanny in *Mansfield Park*), too clever by half (Constantia Durham in *The Egoist*), or little geese (Dora in *David Copperfield*), silly flirts or innocent beyond belief. It is understandable that they should be an awkward subject for the novelist to deal with, for at that tender age the personality is undeveloped. Similarly a painter can only make a face interesting when the vicissitudes of life, thought, love and suffering have given it character. In the portrait of a girl the best he can do is to represent the charm and beauty of youth. But Natasha is entirely natural. She is sweet, sensitive and sympathetic, wilful, childish, already womanly idealistic, quick-tempered, warm-hearted, headstrong, capricious and in everything enchanting. Tolstoy created many women and they are wonderfully true to life, but never another who wins the affection of the reader as does Natasha.

In so long a book as *War and Peace,* and one that took so long to write, it is inevitable that the author's verve should sometimes fail him. I have already remarked that Pierre's adventure into Freemasonry is tedious, and toward the end of his novel Tolstoy seems to me to have somewhat lost interest in his characters. He had conceived a philosophy of history which may be stated as follows: he believed that it was not, as commonly thought, great men who affected its course, but an obscure force that ran through the peoples and drove them unconsciously to victory or defeat. Alexander, Cæsar, Napoleon were no more than figureheads, symbols as it were, who were carried on by a momentum they could neither resist nor control. It was not by his strategy nor his big battalions that Napoleon won his battles, for his orders were not obeyed, either because the situation had changed or they were not delivered in time, but because the enemy was seized with a conviction that the battle was lost and so abandoned the field. For Tolstoy the hero of the invasion of Russia was the Commander-in-Chief, Kutuzov, because he did nothing, avoided battle and merely waited for the French armies to destroy themselves. It may be that as in all Tolstoy's theories there is in this a good deal of truth mingled with a good deal of error, as, for instance, there is in his book *What Is Art,* but I have not the knowledge to deal with the matter. I presume it was to illustrate his idea that he devoted so many chapters to a factual account of the retreat from Moscow. It may be good history, but it is not good fiction.

But if Tolstoy's energies flagged in this last part of his stupendous novel he richly made up for it in the epilogue. It is a brilliant invention. The older novelists were in the habit of telling the reader what happened to their principal characters after the story they had to tell was finished. He was informed that the hero and heroine lived happily, in prosperous circumstances, and had so and so many children, while the villain, if he had not been polished off before the end, was reduced to poverty and married a nagging wife, and so got what he deserved. But it was done perfunctorily, in a page or two, and the reader was left with the impression that it was a sop the author had somewhat contemptuously thrown him. It remained for Tolstoy to make his epilogue a piece of real importance. Seven years have passed and we are taken to the house of Nicholas Rostov, the old Count's son, who has married a rich wife and has children; Pierre and Natasha are paying them a long visit. Natasha is married and she too has children. But the high hopes they had, the eagerness for life, have dwindled away into a dreary, contented quiescence. They love one another, but oh, how dull they have become and how commonplace! After the hazards they have run, the pain and anguish they have suffered they have settled down to a middle-aged complacency. Natasha who was so sweet, so unpredictable, so delightful, is now a fussy housewife. Nicholas Rostov, once so gallant and high spirited, is now a self-opinionated country squire; and Pierre is fatter than ever, good-natured still, but no wiser than he was before. The happy ending is deeply tragic. Tolstoy did not write thus, I think, in bitterness, but because he knew that this is what it would all come to; and he had to tell the truth.

Tolstoy was born in a class that has not often produced writers of eminence. He was the son of Count Nicholas Tolstoy and of Princess Marya Volkonski, an heiress, and he was born, the youngest but one of their five children, at his mother's ancestral home, Yasnaya Polyana. His parents died when he was a child. He was educated first by private tutors, then at the university of Kazan and later at that of St. Petersburg. He was a poor student and took a degree at neither. His aristocratic connections enabled him to enter society, and first at Kazan, then at St. Petersburg and Moscow he went to balls, soirées and parties. He served with the army in the Caucasus and in the Crimean War.

He was at this time a heavy drinker and a reckless gambler; on one occasion, indeed, to pay a gambling debt he had to sell the house on his estate of Yasnaya Polyana which was part of his inheritance. He was a man of strong sexual instincts and while in the Caucasus contracted syphilis. According to his diaries after a night of debauchery, a night with cards or women, or in carousal with gypsies, which if we may judge from their novels is, or was, the usual, but somewhat naive Russian way of having a good time, he suffered pangs of remorse; he did not, however, fail to repeat the performance when the opportunity offered. Though so sturdy that he could walk a whole day or spend ten or twelve hours in the saddle without fatigue, he was small and in appearance unprepossessing. "I knew very well that I was not good looking," he wrote. "There were moments when I was overcome by despair: I imagined that there could be no happiness on earth for one with such a broad nose, such thick lips and such small grey eyes as mine; and I asked God to perform a miracle, and make me handsome, and all I then had, and everything I might have in the future I would have given for a handsome face." He did not know that his homely face revealed a spiritual strength which was wonderfully attractive. He could not see the look of his eyes which gave charm to his expression. At that period he dressed smartly (hoping like poor Stendhal that fashionable clothes would make up for his ugliness) and he was unbecomingly conscious of this rank. A fellow student of his at Kazan wrote of him as follows: "I kept clear of the Count, who from our first meeting repelled one by his assumption of coldness, his bristly hair, and the piercing expression of his half closed eyes. I had never met a young man with such a strange, and to me incomprehensible, air of importance and self satisfaction. . . . He hardly replied to my greetings, as if wishing to intimate that somehow we were far from being equals . . ." And when he joined the army he seems to have held his brother officers in some contempt: "At first," he wrote, "many things in this society shocked me, but I have accustomed myself to them without, however, attaching myself to these gentlemen. I have found a happy mean in which there is neither pride nor familiarity."

While in the Caucasus and afterwards at Sebastopol he wrote a number of sketches and stories and a romanticized account of his childhood and early youth; they were published in a magazine and aroused favorable notice, so that when he went to St. Petersburg from the war he was warmly welcomed. He did not like the people he met there. Nor did they like him. Though convinced of his own sincerity, he could never bring himself to believe in the sincerity of others and had no hesitation in telling them so. He had no patience with accepted opinions. He was irritable, brutally contradictory and arrogantly indifferent to other people's feelings. Turgenev has said that he never met anything more disconcerting than Tolstoy's inquisitorial look, which, accompanied by a few biting words, could goad a man to fury. He took criticism very badly, and when he accidentally read a letter in which there was a slighting reference to himself he immediately sent a challenge to the writer, and his friends had difficulty in preventing him from fighting a ridiculous duel.

At that time there was a wave of liberalism in Russia. The emancipation of the serfs was the pressing question of the day, and Tolstoy, after spending some months of dissipation in the capital, returned to Yasnaya Polyana to put before the peasants on his estates a plan to grant them their freedom, but they suspected there was a catch in it and refused. He started a school for their children. His methods were revolutionary. The pupils had the right not to go to school and even when in school not to listen to their teacher. There was a complete absence of discipline and no one was ever punished. Tolstoy taught, spending the whole day with them, and in the evening joined in their games, told them stories and sang songs with them till late into the night.

About this time he had an affair with the wife of one of his serfs, and a son was born. In later years the bastard, Timothy by name, served as coachman to one of Tolstoy's younger sons. The biographers have found it quaint that Tolstoy's father also had an illegitimate child who also served as coachman to a member of the family. To me it points to a certain moral obtuseness. I should have thought that Tolstoy, with his troublesome conscience, with his earnest desire to raise the serfs from their degraded state, to educate them and teach them to be clean, decent and self-respecting, would have done at least something for his son. Turgenev had an illegitimate child, a daughter, but he took care of her, had governesses to teach her and was deeply concerned with her welfare. Did it cause Tolstoy no embarrassment when he saw the peasant who was his natural son on the box of his legitimate son's carriage?

One of the peculiarities of Tolstoy's temper was that he could embark on a new undertaking with all the enthusiasm in the world, but sooner or later invariably grew bored with it. He somewhat lacked the stolid virtue of perseverance. So after conducting the school for two years, finding the results of his activity disappointing, he closed it. He was tired, dissatisfied with himself and in poor health. He wrote later that at this time he might have despaired had there not been one side of life which lay still unexplored and which promised happiness. This was marriage.

He decided to make the experiment. He was thirty-four. He married Sonya, a girl of eighteen and the second of the two daughters of a Dr. Behrs, who was a fashionable physician in Moscow and an old friend of his family's. They settled down at Yasnaya Polyana. During the first eleven years of their marriage the Countess had eight children and during the next fifteen five more. Tolstoy liked horses and rode well, and he was passionately fond of hunting. He improved his property and bought new estates east of the Volga, so that in the end he owned some sixteen thousand acres of land. His life followed a familiar pattern. There were in Russia scores of noblemen who gambled, got drunk and wenched in their youth, who married and had a flock of children, who settled down on their estates, looked after their property, rode horseback and hunted; and there were not a few who shared Tolstoy's liberal principles and, distressed at the ignorance of the peasants, their dreadful poverty and the squalor in which they lived, sought to ameliorate their lot. The only thing that distinguished him from all of them was that during this time he wrote two of the world's greatest novels, *War and Peace* and *Anna Karenina*. How this came about is a mystery as inexplicable as that the son and heir of a stodgy Sussex squire should have written the *Ode to the West Wind*.

Sonya Tolstoy as a young woman seems to have been attractive. She had a graceful figure, fine eyes, a rather fleshy nose and dark lustrous hair. She had vitality, high spirits and a beautiful speaking voice. Tolstoy had long kept a diary in which he recorded not only his hopes and thoughts, his prayers and self-reproachings, but also the faults, sexual and otherwise, of which he was guilty. On their engagement, in his desire to conceal nothing from his future wife, he gave her his diary to read. She was deeply shocked, but after a sleepless night passed in tears, returned it and forgave. She forgave; she did not forget. They were both violently emotional and had what is known as a lot of character. This generally means that the person thus endowed has some very unpleasant traits. The Countess was exacting, possessive and jealous; Tolstoy was harsh and intolerant. He insisted on her nursing her children, which she was glad to do, but when on the birth of one of them her breasts were so sore that she had to give the child to a wet nurse he was unreasonably angry with her. They quarreled now and then, but made it up. They were very much in love with one another, and on the whole their marriage was a happy one. Tolstoy worked hard and wrote assiduously. His handwriting was often difficult to read, but the Countess, who copied his manuscripts as each portion was written, grew very skilful in deciphering it and was even able to guess the meaning of his hasty jottings and incomplete sentences. She is said to have copied *War and Peace* seven times.

Professor Simmons has thus described his day: "All the family assembled at breakfast, and the master's quips and jokes rendered the conversation gay and lively. Finally he would get up with the words, it's time to work now, and he would disappear into his study, usually carrying a glass of strong tea with him. No one dared disturb him. When he emerged in the early afternoon, it was to take his exercise, usually a walk or a ride. At five he returned for dinner, ate voraciously, and when he had satisfied his hunger he would amuse all present by vivid accounts of any experience he had had on his walk. After dinner he retired to his study to read, and at eight would join the family and any visitors in the living-room for tea. Often there was music, reading aloud or games for the children." *

It was a busy, useful and contented life, and there seemed no reason why it should not run in the same pleasant groove for many years to come, with Sonya bearing children, looking after them and the house, helping her husband in his work, and Tolstoy riding and hunting, superintending his estates and writing books. He was approaching his fiftieth year. That is a dangerous period for men. Youth is past, and looking back, they are apt to ask what their life has amounted to; looking forward, with old age looming ahead, they are apt to find the prospect chilling. And there was one fear that had haunted Tolstoy all his life—the fear of death. Death comes to all men, and most are sensible enough, except in moments of peril or grave illness, not to think of it. But with him it was an ever present malaise. This is how in his book called *Confession* he describes his state of mind at that time: "Five years ago something very strange began to happen to me. At first I experienced moments of perplexity and arrest of life, as though I did not know how to live or what to do; and I felt lost and became dejected. But this passed and I went on living as before. Then these moments of perplexity recurred oftener and oftener and always in the same form. They were always expressed by the questions: What is it for? What does it lead to? I felt that what I had been standing on had broken down and that I had nothing left under my feet. What I had lived on no longer existed, and I had nothing left to live on. My life came to a standstill. I could breathe, eat, drink and sleep, and I could not help doing these things; but there was no life, for there were no wishes the fulfilment of which I could consider reasonable.

* *Leo Tolstoy.* Ernest J. Simmons.

"And all this befell me at a time when all around me I had what is considered complete good fortune. I was not yet fifty; I had a good wife who loved me and whom I loved; good children, and a large estate which without much effort on my part improved and increased. . . . I was praised by people, and without much self-deception could consider that my name was famous. . . . I enjoyed a strength of mind and body such as I have seldom met among men of my kind: physically I could keep pace with the peasants at mowing, and mentally I could work for eight to ten hours at a stretch without experiencing any ill results from such exertion.

"My mental condition presented itself to me in this way: My life is a stupid and spiteful joke that someone has played on me."

When still a boy he had ceased to believe in God, but his loss of faith left him unhappy and dissatisfied, for he had no theory that enabled him to solve the riddle of life. He asked himself, "Why do I live and how ought I to live?" He found no answer. Now he came once more to believe in God, but, strangely enough for a man of so emotional a temper, by a process of reasoning. "If I exist," he wrote, "there must be some cause of it, and a cause of causes. And that first cause of all is what men call God." It is one of the oldest proofs of God's existence. He did not believe in a personal God nor, at that time, in life after death; though later, when he came to think that the Self was part of the Infinite it seemed inconceivable to him that it should cease with the death of the body. For a while he clung to the Russian Orthodox Church, but he was repelled by the fact that the lives of its learned men did not correspond with their principles, and he found it impossible to believe all they required him to believe. He was prepared to accept only what was true in a plain, literal sense. He began to draw near to the believers among the poor and simple and unlettered, and the more he looked into their lives the more convinced he became that, notwithstanding the darkness of their superstition, they had a real faith which was a necessity to them and alone, by giving their life a meaning, made it possible for them to live.

It was years before he arrived at the final determination of his views, and they were years of anguish, meditation and study. It is difficult to summarize these views both briefly and fairly, and I attempt to do so only with hesitation. Rejecting the sacraments since they were based on nothing in Christ's teaching and served only to obscure the truth; rejecting as evident absurdities and an insult to the human intelligence the creeds in which the tenets of Christianity are set forth; he came to believe that the truth was to be found only in the words of Jesus. He believed that the essence of His teaching lay in the precept: *Resist not evil;* the commandment: *Swear not at all,* he decided applied not only to common expletives, but to oaths of any kind, those taken in the witness box by soldiers being sworn in; while the charge: *Love your enemies, bless them that curse you,* forbade men to fight their country's enemies or to defend themselves when attacked. But to adopt opinions with him was to act: if he had come to the conclusion that the substance of Christianity was love, humility, self-denial and the returning of good for evil, it was incumbent upon him, he felt, to renounce the pleasures of life, to labor, to humble himself, to suffer and be merciful.

Sonya Tolstoy, a pious member of the Orthodox Church, insisted that her children have religious instruction, and in every way did her duty in that state of life in which Providence had been pleased to place her. She was not a woman of great spirituality; indeed, what with bearing so many children, nursing them herself, seeing that they were properly educated and running a great household, she had little time for it. She neither understood nor sympathized with her husband's altered outlook, but she accepted it tolerantly enough. When, however, his change of heart resulted in a change of behavior, she was annoyed and did not hesitate to show it. Now that he thought it his duty to consume as little as possible of the work of others, he heated his own stove, fetched water and attended to his clothes himself. With the idea of earning his bread with his own hands he got a shoemaker to teach him to make boots. At Yasnaya Polyana he worked with the peasants, plowing, carting hay and cutting wood; the Countess disapproved, for it seemed to her that from morning till evening he was doing unprofitable physical work which even among the peasants was done by young people.

"Of course you will say," she wrote to him, "that to live so accords with your convictions and that you enjoy it. That is another matter and I can only say: enjoy yourself! But all the same I am annoyed that such mental strength should be lost at log-splitting, lighting samovars and making boots—which are all excellent as a rest or a change of occupation; but not as a special employment." Here she was talking good sense. It was a stupidity on Tolstoy's part to suppose that manual labor is in any way nobler than mental labor. Even if he thought that to write novels for idle people to read was wrong, it is hard to believe that he couldn't have found a more intelligent employment than to make boots, which he made badly and which the people to whom he gave them could not wear. He took to dressing like a peasant and became dirty and untidy. There is a story of how he came in to dinner one day after loading manure, and the stench he brought in with him was such that the windows had to be opened. He gave up hunting, to which he had been passionately addicted, and so that animals should not be killed for the table became a vegetarian. For many years he had been a very moderate drinker, but now he became a total abstainer, and in the end, at the cost of a bitter struggle, left off smoking.

By this time the children were growing up, and for the sake of their education, and because Tanya, the eldest daughter, would be coming out, the Countess insisted that the family should go to Moscow in the winter. Tolstoy disliked city life, but yielded to his wife's determination. In Moscow he was appalled by the contrast he saw between the riches of the rich and the poverty of the poor. "I felt and feel, and shall not cease to feel," he wrote, "that as long as I have any superfluous food and some have none, and I have two coats and some one else has none, I share in a constantly repeated crime." It was in vain for people to tell him that there had always been rich and poor, and always would be; he felt it was not right; and after visiting a night lodging house for the destitute, and seeing its horrors, it shamed him to go home and sit down to a five-course dinner served by two men-servants in dress-clothes and with white ties and white gloves. He tried giving money to the down-and-outs who appealed to him in their need, but came to the conclusion that the money they wheedled out of him did more harm than good. "Money is an evil," he said. "And therefore he who gives money does evil." From this it was a short step to the conviction that property was immoral and to possess it was wrong.

For such a man as Tolstoy the next step was obvious: he decided to rid himself of everything he owned; but here he came into violent conflict with his wife, who had no wish either to beggar herself or to leave her children pennilesss. She threatened to appeal to the courts to have him declared incompetent to manage his affairs, and after heaven only knows how much acrimonious argument he offered to turn his property over to her. This she refused, and in the end he divided it among her and the children. On more than one occasion during the years this dispute lasted he left home to live among the peasants, but before he had gone far was drawn back by the pain he knew he was causing his wife. He continued to live at Yasnaya Polyana and, though mortified by the luxury, luxury on a very modest scale, that surrounded him, none the less profited by it. The friction continued. He disapproved of the conventional education the Countess was giving their children and he could not forgive her for having prevented him from disposing of his property as he wished.

Tolstoy lived for thirty years after his conversion and I have not the space to deal with this long period in detail. I am constrained to omit much that is in itself not without interest. He became a public figure, not only recognized as the greatest writer in Russia, but with an immense reputation throughout the world as a novelist, a teacher and a moralist. Colonies were founded by people who wished to lead their lives according to his views. They came to grief when they tried to put into practice his principle of nonresistance, and the story of their misadventures is both instructive and comic. Owing to Tolstoy's suspicious nature, his harsh argumentativeness, his intolerance and his unconcealed conviction that if others disagreed with him it was from unworthy motives, he retained few friends; but with his increasing fame a host of students, pilgrims visiting the holy places of Russia, sight-seers, admirers and disciples, rich and poor, nobles and commoners, came to Yasnaya Polyana.

Sonya Tolstoy was, as I have said, jealous and possessive, she had always wanted to monopolize her husband, and she resented the invasion of her home by strangers. Her patience was sorely tried: "While describing and relating to people all his fine feelings," she wrote, "and becoming sentimental about himself, he has lived as always, loving sweet food, a bicycle, horseback riding and lust." And on another occasion she wrote in her diary: "I cannot help complaining because all these things he practices for the happiness of people complicate life so much that it becomes more and more difficult for me to live. His vegetarianism means having to cook a double dinner which causes more expense and more work for people. His sermons on love and the good have resulted in indifference to his family and the intrusion of all kinds of rabble into our circle."

One of the first persons to share Tolstoy's views was a young man called Chertkov. He was wealthy and had been a captain in the Guards, but when he came to entertain a belief in the principle of nonresistance he resigned his commission. He was an honest man, an idealist and an enthusiast, but of a domineering temper, with a singular capacity for enforcing his will on others; and Aylmer Maude states that everybody connected with him became his instrument, quarreled with him or had to escape. An attachment sprang up between him and Tolstoy, which lasted till the latter's death, and he acquired an influence over him which bitterly incensed the Countess.

While to most of Tolstoy's friends his views seemed extreme, Chertkov constantly urged him to go further and apply them more rigidly. Tolstoy had been so occupied with his spiritual development that he had neglected his estates, with the result that, though worth something like three hundred thousand dollars, they brought in no more than twenty-five hundred a year. It was evidently not enough to keep the household going and educate a swarm of children. The Countess persuaded her husband to give her the publishing rights of everything he had written before 1881 and on borrowed money started a business of her own to publish his books. It prospered so well that she was able to meet her commitments. But it was obviously incompatible with Tolstoy's belief that property was immoral to retain rights on his literary productions, and when Chertkov gained this ascendancy over him he induced him to declare that everything he had written since 1881 was in the public domain and could be published by anyone. This was enough to anger the Countess, but Tolstoy did more than that; he urged her to surrender her rights over his earlier books, including of course the very popular novels, and this she absolutely refused to do. Her livelihood and that of her family depended upon them. Disputes, acrimonious and protracted, ensued. Sonya and Chertkov gave him little peace. He was torn between conflicting claims neither of which he felt it right to repudiate.

In 1896 Tolstoy was sixty-eight. He had been married for thirty-four years, most of his children were grown up, his second daughter was going to be married; and his wife, at the age of fifty-two, fell ignominiously in love with a man many years younger than herself, a composer called Tanaev. Tolstoy was shocked, ashamed and indignant. Here is a letter he wrote to her: "Your intimacy with Tanaev disgusts me and I cannot tolerate it calmly. If I go on living with you on these terms, I shall only be shortening and poisoning my life. For a year now I have not been living at all. You know this. I have told it to you in exasperations and with prayers. Lately I have tried silence. I have tried everything and nothing is any use. The intimacy goes on and I can see that it may well go on like this to the end. I cannot stand it any longer. It is obvious that you cannot give it up, only one thing remains—to part. I have firmly made up my mind to do this. But I must consider the best way of doing it. I think the very best thing would be for me to go abroad. We shall think out what would be for the best. One thing is certain—we cannot go on like this."

But they did not part; they continued to make life intolerable to one another. The Countess pursued the composer with the fury of an aging woman in love, and he may at first have been flattered, but he soon grew tired of a passion which he could not reciprocate and which made him ridiculous. She realized at last that he was avoiding her, and finally he put a public affront on her that deeply mortified her. Shortly afterwards she came to the conclusion that Tanaev was "thick-skinned and gross both in body and spirit," and the undignified affair came to an end.

The disagreement between husband and wife was by then become common knowledge, and it was a source of bitterness to Sonya that his disciples, now his only friends, sided with him and, because she prevented him from acting as they thought he should, regarded her with hostility. His conversion had brought him little happiness. It had lost him his friends, created discord in his family and caused dissension between his wife and himself. His followers reproached him because he continued to live a life of ease, and indeed he felt himself to blame. He wrote in his diary: "So, I, who am now entering upon my seventieth year, long with all the strength of my spirit for tranquillity and solitude, and though not perfect accord, still something better than this crying disharmony between my life and my beliefs and conscience."

His health gave way. During the next ten years he had several illnesses, one so serious that he nearly died. Gorky, who knew him during this period, describes him as very lean, small and gray, but with eyes keener than ever and a glance more piercing. His face was deeply lined, and he had a long, straggly white beard. He was an old man. He was eighty. A year passed and another. He was eighty-two. He was failing rapidly and it was evident that he had only a few more months to live. They were embittered by sordid quarrels. Chertkov, who apparently did not altogether share Tolstoy's notion that property was immoral, had bought an estate near Yasnaya Polyana, and this naturally facilitated intercourse between the two men. He now pressed Tolstoy to carry into effect his desire that on his death all his works should go into the public domain. The Countess was outraged that she should be deprived of control over the novels which Tolstoy had handed over to her twenty-five years before. The enmity that had long existed between Chertkov and herself burst into open warfare. The children, with the exception of Alexandra, Tolstoy's youngest daughter, who was completely under Chertkov's domination, sided with their mother; they had no wish to lead the sort of life he wanted them to lead and though he had divided his estates among them, saw no reason why they should be deprived of the large sums his writings brought in. But notwithstanding the pressure his family brought upon him, Tolstoy made a will in which he bequeathed all works to the public, and declared that the manuscripts extant at the time of his death should be handed to Chertkov so that he might make them freely accessible to all who might want to publish them. But this was apparently not legal, and

Chertkov urged Tolstoy to have another will drawn up. Witnesses were smuggled into the house, so that the Countess should not know what was going on, and Tolstoy copied the document in his own handwriting behind the locked doors of his study. In this will the copyrights were given to his daughter Alexandra, whom Chertkov had suggested as a nominee, for, as he wrote with some understatement: "I felt certain that Tolstoy's wife and children would not like to see someone not a member of the family made the official legatee." As the will deprived them of their chief means of subsistence that is credible. But this will again did not satisfy Chertkov, and he drew up another himself which Tolstoy copied, sitting on the stump of a tree in the forest near Chertkov's house. This left Chertkov in full control of the manuscripts.

The most important of these were Tolstoy's later diaries. Both husband and wife had long been in the habit of keeping diaries, and it was an understood thing that each should have access to the other's whenever he chose. It was an unfortunate arrangement since the complaints each made of the other when read over gave rise to bitter recrimination. The earlier diaries were in Sonya's hands, but those of the last ten years Tolstoy had delivered to Chertkov. She was determined to get them back, partly because they could eventually be published at a profit, but more because Tolstoy had been very frank in his account of their disagreements and she did not want these passages to be made public. She sent a messenger to Cherkov asking him to give them back. He refused. She threatened upon this to poison or drown herself if they were not returned, and Tolstoy, shattered by the scene she made, took them away from Chertkov, but instead of giving them to her, put them in the bank. Chertkov wrote him a letter on which Tolstoy commented as follows in his diary: "I have received a letter from Chertkov full of reproaches and accusations. They tear me to pieces. Sometimes the idea occurs to me to go far away from them all."

Almost from his youth up Tolstoy had had the desire to leave the world, with its turmoil and trouble, and retire to some place where he could devote himself in solitude to self-perfection; and like many another author he lent his own longing to the two characters in his

novels, Pierre in *War and Peace,* Lévin in *Anna Karenina,*
into whom he put most of himself. The circumstances of
his life at this time combined to give this desire almost
the force of an obsession. His wife, his children tormented him. He was harassed by the disapproval of his
friends who felt that he should at last carry his principles
into complete effect. Many of them were pained because
he did not practice what he preached. Every day he received wounding letters accusing him of hypocrisy. One
eager disciple wrote to beg him to abandon his estate,
give his property to his relations and the poor, leave himself without a kopek and go as a mendicant from town
to town. Tolstoy wrote in reply: "Your letter has profoundly moved me. What you advise me has been my
sacred dream, but up to this time I have been unable to
do it. There are many reasons . . . but the chief reason
is that my doing this must not affect others." People
often thrust into the background of their unconscious
the real reason for their conduct, and in this case I think
the real reason why Tolstoy did not act as both his
friends and his conscience urged him to was simply that
he didn't want to quite enough to do it. There is a point
in the writer's psychology that I have never seen mentioned, though it must be obvious to anyone who has
studied the lives of authors. Every creative writer's work
is, to some extent at least, a sublimation of instincts, desires, daydreams, call them what you like, which for one
cause or another he has repressed, and by giving them
literary expression he is freed of the compulsion to give
them the further release of action. But it is not a complete satisfaction. He is left with a feeling of inadequacy.
That is the ground of the man of letters' glorification of
the man of action and the unwilling, envious admiration
with which he regards him. It may well be that Tolstoy
engaged in manual labor in substitution for his rejected
impulses. It is possible that he would have found in himself the strength to do what he sincerely thought right if
he had not by writing his books taken the edge off his
determination.

He was of course a born writer, and it was his instinct
to put matters in the most effective, dramatic and interesting way he could. I suggest that in his didactic works,
to make his points more telling, he let his pen run away
with him and put his theories in a more uncompromising

fashion than he would have done if he had stopped to
think what consequences they entailed. On one occasion
he did allow that compromise, inadmissible in theory,
was inevitable in practice. But then surely he gave his
whole position away, for if compromise is inevitable in
practice, which means only that the theory is imprac-
ticable, then something must be wrong with the theory.
But unfortunately for Tolstoy the friends, the followers
who came to Yasnaya Polyana in adoring droves could
not reconcile themselves with the notion that their idol
should condescend to compromise. There is indeed something brutal in the persistence with which they pressed
the old man to sacrifice himself to their sense of dramatic
propriety. He was the prisoner of his message. His
writings and the effect they had on so many, for not a
few a disastrous effect, the adoration, the respect, the
affection in which he was held had forced him into a
position from which there was only one issue, and he
could not bring himself to take it.

For when at length he left home on the disastrous but
celebrated journey which ended in his death it was not
because he had at last decided to take the step which his
conscience and the representations of his friends urged
him to take, but to get away from his wife. The immediate cause of his action was fortuitous. He had gone to
bed and after a while he heard Sonya rummaging among
the papers in his study. The secrecy with which he had
made his will preyed upon his mind, and it may be that
he thought then that she had somehow learned of its
existence and was looking for it. When she had gone,
he got up, took some manuscripts, packed some clothes
and, having roused the doctor who had been for some
time living in the house, told him that he was leaving
home. Alexandra was awakened, the coachman was
hauled out of bed, the horses were harnessed, and he
drove, accompanied by the doctor, to the station. It
was five in the morning. The train was crowded and he
had to stand on the open platform at the end of the
carriage in the cold and rain. He stopped first at
Shamardin where his sister was a nun at the convent,
and there Alexandra joined him. She brought the news
that the Countess on finding that Tolstoy was gone had
tried to commit suicide. She had done this more than
once, but as she took little pains to keep her intention to

herself the attempts resulted not in tragedy but only in fuss and bother. Alexandra pressed him to move on in case her mother discovered where he was and followed him. They set out for Rostov-on-Don. He had caught cold and was far from well; in the train he grew so ill that the doctor decided they must stop at the next station. This was at a place called Astapovo. The station-master, hearing who the sick man was, put his house at his disposal.

Next day Tolstoy telegraphed for Chertkov, and Alexandra sent for her eldest brother and asked him to bring a doctor from Moscow. But Tolstoy was too great a figure for his movements to remain unknown, and within twenty-four hours a newspaper man told the Countess where he was. With those of her children who were at Yasnaya Polyana she hastened to Astapovo, but he was so ill by then that it was thought better to keep him in ignorance of her arrival, and she was not allowed to enter the house. The news of his illness created world-wide concern. During the week it lasted the station at Astapovo was thronged by representatives of the Government, police officers, railway officials, pressmen, photographers and many others. They lived in railway carriages sidetracked for their accommodation, and the local telegraph office could hardly cope with the work put on it. Tolstoy was dying in a blaze of publicity. More doctors arrived till at last there were five to attend him. He was often delirious, but in his lucid moments worried about Sonya whom he still believed to be at home and unaware of his whereabouts. He knew he was going to die. He had feared death all his life; he feared it no longer. "This is the end," he said, "and it doesn't matter." He grew worse. In his delirium he continued to cry out: "To escape! To escape!" At last Sonya was admitted into the room. He was unconscious. She fell to her knees and kissed his hand; he sighed, but gave no sign that he knew she had come. A few minutes after six in the morning, on Sunday, November 7, 1910, he died.

In order to write this article I have quoted largely from Aylmer Maude's *Life of Tolstoy* and I have used his translation of *Confession*. Maude had the advantage of knowing Tolstoy and his family, and his narrative is very readable. It is unfortunate that he should have thought fit to tell more about himself and his opinions than most people can want to know. I am also deeply indebted to Professor Simmons's full, detailed and convincing biography. He gives many interesting facts which Aylmer Maude, presumably from discretion, omitted. It must long remain the standard biography in English.

HONORÉ DE BALZAC
and
OLD MAN GORIOT

As I SAID at the beginning of my introduction to *War and Peace,* of all the great novelists that have enriched with their works the spiritual treasures of the world, Balzac is to my mind the greatest. He had genius. There are writers who have achieved fame on the strength of one or two books; sometimes because from the mass they have written only a fragment has proved of enduring value; sometimes because their inspiration, growing out of a singular experience or owing to a peculiarity of temper, only served for a production of little bulk. They say their say once for all, and if they write again repeat themselves. Fertility is a merit in a writer, and Balzac's fertility was prodigious. His field was the whole life of his time and his range as extensive as the frontiers of his country. His knowledge of men was vast, but in some directions less exact than in others, and he knew the middle class of society, doctors, lawyers, clerks and journalists, shopkeepers, village priests better than he knew either the great world or the world of the city workers or the tillers of the soil. Like all novelists he wrote of the wicked more successfully than of the good. His observation was precise and minute. His invention was stupendous, and the list of characters he created is staggering.

But I don't believe he was a very interesting man. There were no great complications in his character, no puzzling contradictions and no intricate subtleties. He was in fact rather obvious. I am not sure even that he was very intelligent; his ideas were commonplace and superficial. But he had a power of creation that was extraordinary. He was like a force of nature, a tumultuous river, for instance, overflowing its banks and sweeping everything before it, or a hurricane blustering its wild way across quiet country places or through the streets of populous cities. As a painter of society his distinctive gift was not only to envisage men in their relations to one another—all novelists except the writers of adventure stories pure and simple do that—but also and especially in their relations to the world they live in. Most novelists take a group of persons, sometimes no more than two or three, and treat them as though they lived under a glass case. It often produces an effect of intensity, but at the same time unfortunately one of artificiality. People do not only live in their own lives, but in the lives of others: in their own they play leading parts, but in those of others sometimes important, but it may be also very small ones. You go to the barber's to get your hair cut, it means nothing to you, but it may conceivably be a turning point in the barber's life. By realizing all that this implies, Balzac was able to give a vivid and exciting impression of multifariousness of life, its confusions and cross-purposes, and of the remoteness of the causes that result in significant effects. I think he was the first novelist to notice the importance of economics in everybody's life. He would not have thought it enough to say that money is the root of all evil, he thought the desire for money, the appetite for money, was the mainspring of human action. Money and ever more money is the obsession of character after character in his novels. Their aim is to live in splendor, to have fine houses, fine horses, fine women; and all means to get what they want are good so long as they succeed. It is a vulgar aim, but I don't suppose it is less common in our day than it was in his.

If you had met Balzac in his early thirties, when he was already successful, this is the man you would have seen, a little fellow, already on the fat side, with powerful shoulders and a massive chest, so that he would not have struck you as small; with a neck like a bull's, its whiteness contrasting with the redness of his face, and thick, smiling lips, noticeably red. His nose was square, with wide nostrils, his brow noble; his hair, dense and black, swept back on his skull like a lion's mane. His brown eyes, flecked with gold, had a life, a light, a magnetism that were extraordinary; they obscured the fact that his features were irregular and common. His expression was jovial, frank and good-natured. His vitality was abounding so that you would have felt it exhilarating merely to be in his presence. Then you might have been struck by the beauty of his hands. He was very proud of them. They were like a bishop's, small, white and fleshy, and the nails were rosy. If you had met him in the evening you would have found him dressed in a blue coat with gold buttons, black pants, a white vest, black silk openwork socks, patent leather shoes, fine white linen and yellow gloves. But if you ran across him in the daytime you would have been surprised to see him in a shabby old coat, his pants muddy, his shoes uncleaned, and in a shocking old hat.

His contemporaries are agreed that at this time he was naive, childish, kindly and genial. George Sand has said that he was sincere to the point of modesty, boastful to the point of braggadocio, confident, expansive, very good and quite crazy, drunk on water, intemperate in work and sober in other passions, equally matter of fact and romantic, credulous and skeptical, puzzling and contrary.

The novelist's real name was Balssa, and his ancestors were farm-laborers; but his father, a pettifogging attorney, having after the revolution come up in the world, changed his name to Balzac. He married an heiress, and Honoré, the eldest of his four children, was born in 1799 at Tours where his father was administrator of the hospital. After some years at school, where he was bad and idle, he entered a lawyer's office in Paris, whither his father had been moved, but when, three years later, after he had passed the necessary examinations it was proposed that he should make the law his profession, he rebelled. He wanted to be a writer. There were violent family scenes. At last, notwithstanding the continued opposition of his mother, a severe practical woman whom he never liked, his father yielded so far as to give him a chance. He was to live by himself with an allowance just large enough to provide a bare subsistence, and try his luck.

The first thing he did was to write a tragedy on Cromwell. He read it to his assembled family. They agreed that it was worthless. It was then sent to a professor whose verdict was that the author should do whatever else he liked, but not write. Angry and discouraged, Balzac decided, since he could not be a tragic poet, to be a novelist, and he wrote two or three novels inspired by Walter Scott, Anne Radcliffe and Byron. But his family had come to the conclusion that the experience had failed, and they ordered him to come home by the first stagecoach. Balzac the elder had retired, and they were living, not far from Paris, in a village called Villeparisis. A friend of his, a hack writer, came to see him there and urged him to write another novel. He set to work. So began a long series of potboilers which he wrote sometimes alone, sometimes in collaboration, under a number of pseudonyms. No one knows how many books he turned out between 1821 and 1825. Some authorites claim as many as fifty. They were for the most part historical, for then Walter Scott was at the height of his renown, and they were designed to cash in on his fantastic vogue. They were very bad, but they had their use in teaching Balzac the value of swift action to hold the reader's attention and the value of dealing with the subjects that people regard as of primary importance; love, wealth, honor and life. It may be that they taught him too what his own proclivities must also have suggested to him, that to be read the author must concern himself with passion. Passion may be base, trivial or unnatural, but if violent enough is not without some trace of grandeur.

While he was living at Villeparisis with his family, Balzac made the acquaintance of a neighbor, a Madame de Berny, the daughter of a German musician who had been in the service of Marie Antoinette, and of one of her maids. She was forty-five. Her husband was sickly and querulous. She had had eight children by him and one by a lover. She became Balzac's friend, then his mistress, and remained his friend till her death fourteen years later. It was a strange relation. He loved her as a lover, but he transferred to her besides all the love he had never felt for his mother. She was not only a mistress, but a devoted friend whose advice, encouragement, help and disinterested affection were always his for the asking. But the affair gave rise to scandal in the village, and Madame Balzac, as was natural, did not approve of her son's entanglement with a woman old enough to be his mother. His books, moreover, brought in very little money, and she was concerned about his future. A friend suggested that he should go into business, and the idea seemed to have appealed to him. Madame de Berny put up forty-five thousand francs, nine thousand dollars, which then represented three or four times that amount;

and with a couple of partners he became a publisher, a printer and a type founder. He was not a businessman. He was wildly extravagant. He charged up to the firm his personal expenditure with tailors, bootmakers, jewelers and even laundrymen. At the end of three years the firm went into liquidation, and his mother had to provide fifty thousand francs in order to pay his creditors. The The disastrous experience, however, provided him with a lot of special information and a knowledge of practical life which were useful to him in the novels he afterwards wrote.

After the crash he went to stay with friends in Brittany, and there got the material for a novel, *Les Chouans,* which was his first serious work and the first which he signed with his own name. He was thirty. From then on he wrote with frenzied industry till his death twenty-one years later. The number of books, long and short, that he wrote is astounding. Every year he produced one or two long novels and a dozen novelettes and short stories. Besides this he wrote a number of plays, some of which were never accepted, and of those that were all, with one exception, lamentably failed; and for a brief period he ran a paper which appeared twice a week and most of which he wrote himself.

He was a great note-taker. Wherever he went he took his notebook, and when he happened upon something that might be useful to him, hit upon an idea of his own or was taken with someone else's, he jotted it down. When possible he visited the scene of his stories, and sometimes took considerable journeys to see a street or a house that he wanted to describe. Like all novelists, I think, his characters were modeled on people he had known, but by the time he had exercised his imagination upon them they were to all intents and purposes creatures of his own imagination. He took a lot of trouble over their names, for he had the notion that the name should correspond with the character and look of the individual who bore it.

When at work he led a chaste and regular life. He went to bed soon after his evening meal and was wakened by his servant at one. He got up, put on his white robe, spotless, for he claimed that to write one should be clad in garments without spot or stain, and then by candlelight, fortifying himself with cup after cup of black coffee, wrote with a quill from a raven's wing. He stopped writing at seven, took a bath and lay down. Between eight and nine his publisher came to bring him proofs or to get a piece of manuscript from him; then he set to work again till noon when he ate boiled eggs, drank water and had more coffee; he worked till six, when he had his light dinner which he washed down with a little Vouvray. Sometimes a friend or two would come in, but after a little conversation he went to bed.

He was not a writer who knew what he wanted to say from the start. He began with a rough draft, which he rewrote and corrected, changing the order of chapters, cutting, adding, altering; and finally sent to the printers a manuscript which it was almost impossible to decipher. The proof was returned to him, and this he treated as if it were only an outline of the projected work. He not only added words, he added sentences, not only sentences, but paragraphs, and not only paragraphs but chapters. When his proofs were set up once more with all the alterations and corrections and a fair set delivered to him, he went to work on them again, and made more changes. Only after this would he consent to publication and then only on condition that in a future edition he should be allowed to make further revisions and improvements. The expense of all this was naturally great and resulted in constant quarrels with his publishers.

The story of his relations with editors and publishers is long, dull and sordid, and I will deal with it, as shortly as I can, only because it had an influence on his life and work. He was more than a trifle unscrupulous. He would get an advance on a book and guarantee to deliver it on a certain date and then, tempted by quick money, would stop writing it to give to another editor or publisher a novel or a story he had written posthaste. Actions were brought against him for breach of contract, and the costs and damages he had to pay greatly increased his already heavy debts. For no sooner did success come to him, bringing him contracts for books he was engaged to write (and sometimes never did) than he moved into a spacious apartment, which he furnished at great expense, and bought a cabriolet and a pair of horses. He must have been one of the first persons to conceive a passion for interior decoration, and the description of his various establishments is as magnificent as it is tasteless. He hired a groom, a cook and a manservant, bought clothes for himself and a livery for his groom, and quantities of plate which he had embossed with arms which did not belong to him. They were those of an old family of the name of Balzac, and he assumed them when he added the *de,* the *particule,* to his own name to make believe that he was of noble birth. To pay for all this grandeur he borrowed from his sister, his friends, and his publishers, and signed bills that he kept on renewing. His debts continued to increase, but he continued to buy—porcelain, cabinets, pieces of Buhl, pictures, statues, jewelry; he had his books bound gorgeously in morocco, and one of his many canes was studded with turquoises. For one dinner he gave he had his dining room refurnished and the decoration entirely changed. In passing I may remark that when alone he ate soberly, but in company his appetite was voracious. One of his publishers declares that at one meal he saw him devour a hundred oysters, twelve cutlets, a duck, a brace of partridges, a sole, a number of desserts and a dozen pears. It is not surprising that in time he became very fat and his belly enormous.

At intervals, when his creditors were more than usually pressing, many of these possessions had to be pawned; now and then the brokers came in, seized his furniture and sold it by public auction. Nothing could cure him. To the end of his life he continued to buy with senseless extravagance. He was a shameless borrower, but so great was the admiration his genius excited, he seldom exhausted the generosity of his friends. Women are not as a rule willing lenders, but Balzac apparently found them easy. He was totally lacking in delicacy, and there is no sign that he had any qualms about taking money from them.

It will be remembered that his mother had cut into her small fortune to save him from bankruptcy; the dowries of her two daughters had further reduced her means, and at last the only property she had left was a house she rented. The time came when she found herself so desperately in need that she wrote a letter to her son which André Billy has quoted in his *Vie de Balzac,* and which I shall translate:

"The last letter I had from you was in November 1834. In it you agreed to give me, from April 1st, 1835, two hundred francs every quarter to help me with my rent and my maid. You understood that I could not live as suited my poverty; you had made your name too conspicuous and your luxury too evident for the difference in our positions not to be shocking. Such a promise as you made me was for you, I think, an admitted debt. It is now April 1837, which means that you owe me for two years. Of these 1600 francs, you gave me last December 500 francs as though they were a charity ungraciously bestowed. Honoré, for two years my life has been a constant nightmare, my expenses have been enormous. You weren't able to help me, I don't doubt it, but the result is that the sums I've borrowed on my house have diminished its value and now I can raise no more, and everything of value I had is in pawn; and that I've at last come to the moment when I have to say to you: 'Bread, my son.' For several weeks I've been eating that which was given me by my good son-in-law, but, Honoré, it can't go on like that: seeing that you have the means to make long and costly journeys of all sorts, costly in money and in reputation—for yours will be cruelly compromised when you come back because of the contracts you have failed to keep—when I think of all this my heart breaks! My son, as you've been able to afford yourself . . . mistresses, mounted canes, rings, silver, furniture, your mother may also without indiscretion ask you to carry out your promise. She has waited to do so till the last moment, but it has come . . ." To this letter he answered: "I think you'd better come to Paris and have an hour's talk with me."

What are we to say to this? His biographer says that since genius has its rights the morality of Balzac should not be judged by ordinary standards. That is a matter of opinion. I think it is better to acknowledge that he was grossly selfish, very unscrupulous and none too honest. The best excuse one can make for his financial shiftiness is that with his buoyant, optimistic temper he was always firmly convinced that he was going to make vast sums out of his writings (for the time he made a great deal) and fabulous amounts out of the speculations which one after another tempted his ardent imagination. But whenever he actually engaged in one the result was to leave him still more heavily in debt. He could never have been the writer he was if he had been sober, practical and thrifty. He was a show-off; he adored luxury, and he could not help spending money. He worked like a dog to fulfil his obligations, but unfortunately, before ever he paid off his more pressing debts, he had contracted new ones. There is one curious fact worth mentioning. It was only under pressure of debt that he could bring himself to write. Then he would work till he was pale and worn out, and in these circumstances he wrote some of his best novels; but when by some miracle he was not in harrowing straits, when the brokers left him in peace, when editors and publishers were not bringing actions, his invention seemed to fail him and he could not bring himself to put pen to paper.

Balzac's literary success brought him, as success does, many new friends; and his immense vitality, his radiant good humor made him a welcome guest in all but the most exclusive salons. One great lady to be attracted by his celebrity was the Marquise de Castries, the daughter of one duke and the niece of another who was a direct descendant of King James the Second of England. She wrote to him under an assumed name, he answered, and she wrote again disclosing her identity. He went to see her; they grew intimate, and presently he went to see her every day. She was pale, blonde and flower-like. He fell in love with her, but though she allowed him to kiss her aristocratic hands she resisted his further advances. He scented himself, he put on new yellow gloves every day; it availed him nothing. He grew impatient and irritable and began to suspect she was playing with him. The fact is plain that she wanted an admirer and not a lover. It was doubtless flattering to have a clever young man, already famous, at her feet, but she had no intention of becoming his mistress. The crisis came at Geneva where, with her uncle, the Duke of Fitz-James, as a chaperon, they were staying on their way to Italy. No one knows exactly what happened. Balzac and the Marquise went for an excursion, and he came back in tears. It may be supposed that he made summary demands on her which she rejected in a manner that deeply mortified him. Pained and angry, feeling himself abominably used, he went back to Paris. But he was not a novelist for nothing; every experience, even the most humiliating, was grist to his mill; and the Marquise de Castries was to serve in future as a model for the heartless flirt of high rank.

While still laying fruitless siege to the great lady Balzac had received a fan letter from Odessa signed *L'Étrangère*. A second, similarly signed, arrived after the break. He put an advertisement in the only French paper allowed to enter Russia: *"M. de B has received the communication sent to him; he has only this day been able by this paper to acknowledge it and regrets that he does not know where to send his reply."* The writer was Eveline Hanska, a Polish lady of noble birth and immense wealth. She was thirty-two, and married, but her husband was much older. She had had five children, but only one, a girl, was living. She saw Balzac's advertisement and so arranged that she might receive his letters if he wrote to her in care of a bookseller at Odessa. A correspondence ensued.

Thus began the great passion of Balzac's life.

The letters the pair exchanged grew more intimate. In the rather exaggerated manner of the time Balzac laid bare his heart in such a way as to arouse the lady's pity and sympathy. She was romantic, and bored with the monotony of domestic life in the great chateau in the Ukraine in the middle of fifty thousand acres of flat land. She admired the author, she was interested in the man. When they had been exchanging letters for a couple of years Madame Hanska with her husband, who was in bad health, her daughter, a governess and a retinue of servants went to Neufchatel in Switzerland; and there on her invitation Balzac went too. There is a romantic, but possibly apocryphal, account of how they met. Balzac was walking in the public gardens when he saw a lady sitting on a bench reading a book. She dropped her handkerchief, and on picking it up he noticed that the book was one of his. He spoke. It was the woman he had come to see. At this time she was a handsome creature, of somewhat opulent charms; her eyes were fine, though with ever so slight a cast, her hair was beautiful and her mouth lovely. She may have been a trifle taken aback at the first sight of the fat, red-faced man, like a butcher in appearance, who had written her such lyrical and passionate letters, but if she was, the brilliance of his gold-flecked eyes, his abounding vitality, made her forget the shock and in no long time he became her lover. After some weeks he was obliged to go back to Paris, and they parted with the arrangement that they should meet again early in the winter at Geneva. He arrived for Christmas and spent six weeks there during which he wrote *La Duchesse de Langeais,* in which he revenged himself on Madame de Castries for the affront she had made him suffer.

On his return to Paris he met a Countess Guidoboni-Visconti. She was an ash-blonde, voluptuous, an English-woman, notoriously unfaithful to an easy-going husband, and Balzac was immediately fascinated by her. She became his mistress. But the Romantics of those days conducted their love affairs as it were on the front page of a tabloid and it was not long before Madame Hanska, then living in Vienna, heard that her lover was unfaithful. She wrote a letter to him, full of bitter reproaches, in which she announced that she was about to go back to the Ukraine. It was a blow. He had been counting upon marrying her on the death of her husband, an event which he persuaded himself could not be long delayed, and being put in possession of her vast fortune. He borrowed two thousand francs and hurried off to Vienna to make his peace. He traveled as the Marquis de Balzac, with his bogus coat of arms on his luggage, and a valet; this added to the expense of the journey, since as a man of title it was beneath his dignity to haggle with hotel-keepers, and he had to give tips suitable to the rank he had assumed. He arrived penniless. Madame Hanska heaped more reproaches on him, and he was obliged to lie his head off to allay her suspicions. Three weeks later she left for the Ukraine, and they did not meet again for eight years.

Balzac went back to Paris and resumed his relations with the Countess Guidoboni. For her sake he indulged in extravagance wilder than ever. He was arrested for debt, and she paid the sum necessary, a considerable one, to save him from going to prison. Thenceforward from time to time she came to the rescue when his financial situation was desperate. In 1836 to his great grief Madame de Berny, his first mistress, died, and he said of her that she was the only woman he had ever loved: others have said that she was the only woman who had ever loved *him*.

In the same year the blonde Countess informed him that she was with child by him. When it was born, her husband, a tolerant man, remarked: "Well, I knew that

Madame wanted a dark child. So she's got what she wanted." In passing it may be mentioned that in the course of his amorous career the great novelist had by different mistresses one boy and three girls. He seems to have taken singularly little interest in them. Of his other affairs I will only mention one, with a widow called Hélène de Valette, because it began, as had those with the Marquise de Castries and Madame Hanska, by a fan letter. It is odd that three of his five chief love affairs should have started in this way. It may be that that is why they were unsatisfactory. When a woman is attracted to a man by his fame she is too much concerned with the credit she may get through the connection with him to be capable of that blessed something of disinterestedness that genuine love evokes. She is a thwarted exhibitionist who snatches at a chance to gratify her instinct. The affair with Hélène de Valette did not last long, and seems to have come to an end in a dispute over ten thousand francs Balzac had borrowed from her.

At last the moment he had been so long awaiting arrived. Monsieur Hanska died in 1842. At last his dreams were to come true. At last he was going to be rich. At last he was going to be free of his petty, bourgeois debts. But the letter in which Eveline told him of the death of her husband was followed by another in which she told him that she would not marry him. She could not forgive him his infidelities, his extravagance, his debts. He was reduced to despair. She had told him in Vienna that she did not expect him to be physically faithful so long as she had his heart. Well, that she had always had. He was outraged by her injustice. He came to the conclusion that he could only win her back by seeing her, and so, after a good deal of correspondence, notwithstanding her reluctance he made the journey to St. Petersburg where she then was. His calculations proved correct; both were fat and both were middle-aged, he was forty-three and she was forty-two; but it looks as though when with him she could refuse him nothing. They became lovers again, and again she promised to marry him. It was seven years before she kept her promise. The biographers have been puzzled to know why she hesitated so long, but surely the reasons are not far to seek. She was a great lady, proud of her noble lineage; and it is likely enough that she saw a big difference between being the mistress of a cele-

brated author and the wife of a vulgar upstart. Her
family must have done all they could to persuade her not
to contract such an unsuitable alliance. She had a marriageable daughter whom it was her duty to settle in ac-
cordance with her rank and circumstances. Balzac was a
notorious spendthrift; she may well have feared that he
would play ducks and drakes with her fortune. He was
always wanting money from her. He did not dip into her
purse, he plunged both hands into it. She was rich and
herself extravagant, but it is very difficult to fling your
money about for your own pleasure and to have someone else fling it about for his.

The strange thing is not that Eveline Hanska waited
so long to marry Balzac, but that she married him at all.
During those seven years they saw one another from time
to time, and as a result of one of these meetings she became pregnant. Balzac was enchanted. He thought he had
won at last and begged her to marry him at once; but she,
unwilling to have her hand forced, wrote to tell him
that after her confinement she intended to go back to
the Ukraine to economize and would marry him later.
The child was born dead. This was in 1845 or 1846. She
married him in 1850. Balzac had spent the winter with
her in the Ukraine, and the ceremony took place there.

Why did she finally consent? His prolonged and ar-
duous labor had at length shattered his vigorous constitution, and his health was failing. During the winter
he was very ill, and though he recovered it was evident
that he had not long to live. Perhaps she was moved to
pity for a dying man who notwithstanding his infidelities
had loved her so long and constantly; perhaps her con-
fessor, for she was a devout woman, urged her to regular-
ize her unconventional situation. Anyhow she married
him, and they went back to Paris where on her money
he had bought and expensively furnished a large house.
But she was no longer a rich woman. She had dis-
possessed herself of her vast possessions in favor of her
daughter and retained only a moderate annuity. If Balzac was disappointed he made no sign of it. It is lament-
able to have to relate that after all this eager waiting,
when at last his hopes were realized, the marriage was
not a success. Eveline made him unhappy. He fell ill
again, and this time he did not recover. He died on the
17th August, 1850. Eveline was heartbroken, and in a

letter to a friend wrote that now she desired nothing but to rejoin her husband in the world beyond; she consoled herself, however, sufficiently to take as her lover a painter called Jean Gigoux and nicknamed Pou-Gris (Gray louse) on account of his ugliness. He does not appear to have been a good painter.

It is not easy out of Balzac's immense production to choose the novel that best represents him. In almost all there are at least two or three characters that because they are obsessed by a simple, primitive passion stand out with extraordinary force. It was in the depiction of just such characters that his strength lay; when he had to deal with a character of any complexity he was less happy. In almost all his novels there are scenes of great power, and in several an absorbing story. I have chosen *Old Man Goriot* for several reasons. The story it tells is continuously interesting. In some of his novels Balzac interrupts his narrative to discourse upon all kinds of irrelevant matters, but from this defect *Old Man Goriot* is on the whole free. He lets his characters explain themselves by their words and actions as objectively as it was in his nature to do. *Old Man Goriot* is well constructed, and the two threads, the old man's self-sacrificing love for his ungrateful daughters and the ambitious Rastignac's first steps in the crowded, corrupt Paris of his day, are plausibly interwoven. *Old Man Goriot* is interesting also because it was in this novel that Balzac first systematically applied the notion of bringing the same characters into novel after novel. The difficulty is that you must create characters who interest you so much that you want to know what happens to them as their lives go on. Balzac here triumphantly succeeds and, speaking for myself, I read with added enjoyment the novels in which I learn what has become of certain persons, Rastignac for instance, whose future I have been eager to know about. The device is useful because it is an economy of invention, but I don't believe Balzac, with his inexhaustible fertility, resorted to it on that account. I think he felt it added reality to his narrative, for in the ordinary course of events we do have repeated contacts with a fair proportion of the same people; but more than that, I think his main object was to knit his whole work together in a comprehensive unity. His aim was not to depict a group, a set, a class or even a society, but a period and a civilization. He suffered from the delusion, too common to his countrymen, that France, whatever disasters had befallen it, was the center of the universe; but perhaps it was just on that account that he had the self-assurance to create a world, multi-colored, various and profuse, and the power to give it the convincing throb of life.

But this concerns *The Human Comedy* as a whole. Here we are concerned only with *Old Man Goriot*. I believe Balzac to have been the first novelist to use a boarding-house as the setting for a story. It has been used since many times, for it is a convenient way of enabling the author to present together a variety of characters in various predicaments, but I don't know that it has ever been used with such tremendous effect as in *Old Man Goriot*.

Balzac started his novels slowly. His method was to begin with a detailed description of the scene of action. He apparently took so much pleasure in these descriptions that he often tells you more than you want to know. He never learned the art of saying only what has to be said and not saying what needn't be said. Then he tells you what his characters look like, what their dispositions are, their origins, their habits, their ideas and their defects; and only after this sets out to tell his story. His characters are seen through his own exuberant temperament, and their reality is not quite that of real life; they are painted in primary colors, vivid and sometimes garish, and they are more exciting than ordinary people; but they live and breathe; and you believe in them, I think, because Balzac so intensely believed in them himself. In several of his novels a clever, honest doctor called Bianchon appears; when Balzac was dying he said: "Send for Bianchon. Bianchon will save me."

Old Man Goriot is noteworthy also because in it we meet for the first time one of the most thrilling characters Balzac ever created. Vautrin. The type has been reproduced a thousand times, but never with such striking and picturesque force, nor with such convincing realism. Vautrin has a good brain, willpower and immense vitality. It is worth the reader's while to notice how skillfully Balzac, without giving away a secret he wanted to keep till the end of the book, has managed to suggest that there is something sinister in the man. He is jovial, generous and good-natured; he is strong, uncommonly clever, self-possessed; you not only admire him, you sympathize with him, and yet he is strangely frightening. You are fascinated by him, as was Rastignac, the ambitious, well-born young man who comes to Paris to make his way in the world; but you feel in the fellow's company the same instinctive uneasiness as Rastignac felt. Vautrin may be a figure of melodrama, but he is a great creation.

It is generally agreed that Balzac wrote badly. He was a vulgar man (but was not his vulgarity an integral part of his genius?) and his prose was vulgar. It was prolix, pretentious and too often incorrect. Émile Faguet, a very distinguished critic, in his book on Balzac has given a whole chapter to the faults of taste, style, syntax and language of which the author was guilty. And indeed some of them are so gross that it needs no profound knowledge of French to perceive them. They are frankly shocking. Now it is admitted that Charles Dickens wrote English none too well, and I have been told by cultivated Russians that Tolstoy and Dostoevsky wrote Russian very indifferently. It is odd that the four greatest novelists the world has known should have written their respective languages so ill. It looks as though to write well were not an essential part of the novelist's equipment; but that vigor and vitality, imagination, creative force, observation, knowledge of human nature, with an interest in it and sympathy with it, fertility and intelligence are more important. All the same it is better to write well than badly.

HENRY FIELDING

and

TOM JONES

THE DIFFICULTY OF WRITING about Henry Fielding, the man, is that very little is known about him. Arthur Murphy, who wrote a short life of him in 1762, only eight years after his death, as an introduction to an edition of his works, seems to have had no personal acquaintance with him and had so little material that, presumably in order to fill the eighty pages of his essay, he indulged in long and tedious digressions. The facts he tells are few, and subsequent research has shown that they are inaccurate. Later writers have been at pains to show that Fielding was far from the dissolute creature legend has painted, but unfortunately, in making him more respectable they have made him less engaging. They have been inclined to shake their heads over the obvious fact that he was a man of abundant vitality and impetuous appetites. But there is no reason to expect that a man whose books you admire shall be a model of propriety. His moral character makes his books neither better nor worse. Life is the subject matter of the writer of fiction, and to write about it honestly he must partake of its vicissitudes to the full; he will not learn much by looking at it through a keyhole. But really there is no need to whitewash Fielding; his faults, such as they were, were very human, and only a prudish, silly person can be seriously shocked by them.

Fielding was a gentleman born. His father, an officer in the Army who rose to be a general, was the third son of John Fielding, a Canon of Salisbury, and he in turn was the fifth son of the Earl of Desmond. The Desmonds were a younger branch of the family of Denbigh, who flattered themselves that they were descended from the Habsburgs. Gibbon, the Gibbon of the *Decline and Fall,* wrote in his autobiography: "The successors of Charles the Fifth may

58

disclaim their brethren of England; but the romance of *Tom Jones,* that exquisite picture of human manners, will outlive the palace of the Escorial, and the imperial eagle of the House of Austria." It is a fine phrase and it is a pity that the claim of these noble lords has been shown to have no foundation. They spelled their name Feilding and I have read somewhere that on one occasion the then Earl asked Henry Fielding how this came about, whereupon he answered: "I can only suppose it is because my branch of the family learnt to spell before your lordship's."

Fielding's father married Sarah, the daughter of Sir Henry Gould, a judge of the King's Bench, and at his country seat our author was born in 1707. Three years later the Fieldings, who by this time had two daughters, besides Henry, moved to East Stour in Dorsetshire, and there three more girls and a boy were born. Mrs. Fielding died in 1718, and about this time Henry went to Eton. Here he made some valuable friends and if he did not leave, as Arthur Murphy states, "uncommonly well versed in the Greek authors and an early master of the Latin classics," he had learned enough to be able later to pepper his prose with quotations. At the age of eighteen, by when he had presumably left school, he gave promise already of the sort of man he was going to be. He happened to be staying at Lyme Regis with a trusty servant ready to "beat, maim or kill" for his master, and there he fell in love with a Miss Sarah Andrews, whose considerable fortune added to the charm of her beauty, and he concocted a scheme to carry her off, by main force if necessary, and marry her. It was discovered and the young woman was hurried away and safely married off to a more eligible suitor.

This was in 1725. Fielding was of a comely presence; he was over six feet tall, strong and active, with deep-set, dark eyes, a Roman nose, a short upper lip with an ironical curl to it, and a stubborn, prominent chin. He was active and strong; he had an immense power of enjoyment and his constitution was such as to permit a great deal of excess. For all one knows to the contrary, he spent the next two or three years in London indulging in the gaieties of the town as agreeably as a well-connected young man can do when he has good looks and charm of manner. In 1728 he brought out a play called *Love in*

Several Masques. It was something of a success. One can guess, if one likes, that his father brought pressure to bear on him to prepare himself to earn his living less hazardly than by writing for the stage, and he entered the University of Leyden as a student of law. But his father had married again and either would not or could not continue to pay him the allowance he had promised, so after about a year Fielding was obliged to return to England. He was in such straits that, as in his light-hearted way he put it himself, he had no choice but to be a hackney coachman or a hackney writer.

Austin Dobson, who wrote his life for the English Men of Letters series, says that "his inclinations as well as his opportunities led him to the stage." He had the high spirits, the humor, the keen-witted observation of the contemporary scene which are needed by the playwright; and he seems to have had besides some ingenuity and a sense of construction. The "inclinations" of which Austin Dobson speaks may very well mean that he had the vicarious exhibitionism which is part of the playwright's make-up and that he looked upon writing plays as an easy way to make quick money; the "opportunities" may be a delicate way of saying that he was a handsome fellow of exuberant virility had taken the fancy of a popular actress. Between 1730 and 1736 he brought out two or three plays, farce or comedy, every year. The last two were attacks on the political corruption of the times, and the attacks were effective enough to cause the Ministry to pass a Licensing Act which obliged managers to obtain the Lord Chamberlain's license to produce a play. This act still obtains to torment British authors. After this Fielding wrote only rarely for the stage and, when he did, presumably for no other reason than that he was more than usually hard up.

I will not pretend that I have read his plays, but I have flipped through the pages, and the dialogue seems natural and sprightly. The most amusing bit I have come across is the description of a character which, after the fashion of the day, he gives in the list of Dramatis Personae in *Tomb Thumb The Great:* "a woman entirely faultless, save that she is a little given to drink."

It is usual to dismiss Fielding's plays with something like contempt, and doubtless they lack the literary distinction that the critic reading them in his library two hundred years later would like them to have. But plays are written to be acted, not to be read; it is doubtless very well for them to have literary distinction, but it is not that which makes them good plays, it may (and often does) make them less actable. Fielding's plays have by now lost what merit they had, for the drama depends very much on actuality and so is ephemeral, almost as ephemeral as a newspaper; but some merit they must have had, for neither a young man's wish to write plays nor pressure brought to bear by a favorite actress will induce managers to put on play after play unless they please the public. For in this matter the public is the final judge. Unless the manager can gauge their taste he will go bankrupt. Fielding's plays had at least the merit that the public liked to go to see them. He had no illusions about their worth and said himself that he left off writing for the stage when he should have begun. He wrote for money and had no great respect for the understanding of an audience. "When he had contracted to bring on a play, or a farce," says Murphy, "it is well known by many of his friends now living, that he would go home rather late from a tavern and would, the next morning, deliver a scene to the players, written upon the papers which had wrapped the tobacco, in which he so much delighted."

Murphy has another anecdote which shows rather charmingly Fielding's attitude toward the public. During the rehearsals of a comedy called *The Wedding Day,* Garrick, who was playing in it, objected to a scene and asked Fielding to cut it. "No, damn 'em," said Fielding, "if the scene isn't a good one let them find it out." The scene was played, the audience noisily expressed their displeasure, and Garrick retired to the green-room where his author was "indulging his genius, and solacing himself with a bottle of champagne. He had by this time drunk pretty plentifully; and cocking his eye at the actor, with streams of tobacco trickling down from the corner of his mouth, 'What's the matter, Garrick,' says he, 'what are they hissing now?'

" 'Why, the scene that I begged you to retrench; I knew it would not do; and they have so frightened me, that I shall not be able to collect myself the whole night.'

" 'Oh, damn 'em,' replies the author, 'they *have* found it out, have they?' "

If I have dwelt on what was after all not much more than an episode in Fielding's career it is because I think it was important to his development as a novelist. Quite a number of eminent novelists have tried their hands at playwriting, but I cannot think of any that have succeeded. The fact is that the techniques are very different, and to have learned how to write a novel is of no help when it comes to writing a play. The novelist has all the time he wants to develop his theme; he can describe his characters as minutely as he chooses and make their behavior plain to the reader by relating their motives; if he is skilful he can give verisimilitude to improbabilities; if he has a gift for narrative he can gradually work up to a climax which a long preparation makes more striking; he does not have to show action but only to write about it; he can make the persons explain themselves in dialogue for as many pages as he likes. But a play depends on action, and by action of course I don't mean violent action like falling off a precipice or being blown up by a landmine; such an action as handing a person a glass of water may be of the highest dramatic intensity. The power of attention that an audience has is very limited, and it must be held by a constant succession of incidents; something fresh must be doing all the time; the theme must be presented at once and its development must follow a definite line, without digression into irrelevant by-paths; the dialogue must be crisp and pointed, and it must be so put that the listener can catch its meaning without having to stop and think; the characters must be all of a piece, easily grasped by the eye and the understanding, and however complex, their complexity must be plausible. A play cannot afford loose ends; however slight, its foundation must be secure and its structure solid.

When the playwright, who has acquired the qualities which I have suggested are essential to writing a play which audiences will sit through with pleasure, starts writing novels he is at an advantage. He has learned to be brief, he has learned the value of rapid incident, he has learned not to linger on the way, but to stick to his point and get on with his story; he has learned to make his characters display themselves by their words and actions without the help of description; and so, when he comes to work on the larger canvas which the novel allows he can not only profit by the advantages peculiar to the form of the novel, but his training as a playwright will enable him to make his novel lively, swift-moving and dramatic. These are excellent qualities, and some very good novelists, whatever their other merits, have not possessed them. I cannot look upon the years Fielding spent writing plays as wasted; I think on the contrary the experience he gained then was of value to him when he came to writing novels.

While he was still busy with the theater he married Charlotte Cradock. She was one of three sisters who lived at Salisbury, and nothing is known of her but that she was beautiful and charming. Fielding described her in *Sophia,* and the reader of *Tom Jones* can therefore gain a very exact notion of what she looked like in the eyes of her lover and husband. As a husband he was tender and passionate, though since he was what he was, probably none too faithful. He doubtless regretted his infidelities, but that, it may be supposed, did not prevent him from falling for the next pretty woman who came his way. With Charlotte Cradock he got £1500. One authority says it was by way of dowry, another that it was a legacy; anyhow, after the failure of a comedy, with this money he retired to his small estate at East Stour and according to Arthur Murphy there kept open house, had a pack of hounds and a large retinue of servants in "costly yellow liveries." Subsequent biographers have been at pains to show that this story is exaggerated, but the fact remains that by 1736, two years after his marriage, the money was spent and he returned to London to write more plays and to manage a theater in the Haymarket.

When the Licensing Act became a law a year later and so put an end to these activities, he had a wife and child and precious little money to support them on. He had to find a means of livelihood. He entered the Middle Temple and though "it happened that the early taste he had taken of pleasures would occasionally return upon him; and conspire with his spirit and vivacity to carry him into the wild enjoyments of the town," he was in due course called to the bar. He practiced law with proper industry, but the dissipation of his early life had ruined his constitution and like everyone else at the time he suffered severely from the gout. He was thus able to follow his profession only by snatches. He took again to his pen. He wrote political tracts, a play or two and articles for a paper called the *Champion*. In 1742 he produced *Joseph Andrews*. This was his first novel to be published, though not, it is believed, the first he wrote, which was *Jonathan Wild*. It is not my business to discuss his literary work in general, but just now only to tell the little that is known of his life. Shortly after the publication of *Joseph Andrews* his beautiful wife died of fever; she died in his arms and left him distracted with grief. For some years he produced nothing of importance.

He wrote for two papers, the *True Patriot* and the *Jacobite's Journal,* in support of the government, and when they came to an end was granted a pension. But he was improvident and of a naturally extravagant temper and he continued to be in embarrassed circumstances. A story is told of him that is characteristic: in order to pay the tax collector he got his publisher, Andrew Miller, to give him an advance and while taking the money home met a friend who was in even worse case than himself; so he gave him the money and when the tax collector called sent him the message: "Friendship has called for the money and had it; let the collector call again."

Four years after his wife's death he married her maid, Mary Daniel. It shocked his friends, and his cousin Lady Mary Wortley-Montagu, the letter-writer, was haughtily scornful because he could "feel raptures with his cook-maid"; but though she had few personal charms, she was an excellent creature and he never spoke of her but with affection and respect. The second Mrs. Fielding was a very decent woman, who looked after him well, and he wanted some looking after, a good wife and a good mother. She bore her husband two boys and a girl.

Among the friends Fielding has made at Eton, and whose friendship he had retained, was George Lyttelton, a member of a distinguished political family (distinguished to the present day) and a generous patron of literature. He was a Lord of the Treasury from 1744 to 1754, and in 1748 succeeded in getting Fielding made Justice of the Peace for Westminster. He was fitted for the post by his training as a lawyer, his knowledge of life and his natural gifts. He appears to have performed his duties with efficiency. Shortly after his appointment he was chosen Chairman of Quarter Sessions and established himself in Bow Street. Fielding says that before his accession the job was worth £500 a year of dirty money, but that he made no more than £300 a year of clean. In 1749 he published *Tom Jones*. He was paid £700 for it. Since I presume money at that period was worth four to six times what it is worth now, this sum was the equivalent of something between £3000 and £4000. That would not be bad payment for a novel in England today.

But Fielding's health was by now very poor. His attacks of gout were frequent, and he had often to go to Bath or to a cottage he had near London to recuperate. But he did not cease to write. He wrote pamphlets concerning his office; one, an *Enquiry into the Causes of the Late Menace of Robbers,* is said to have helped the famous Gin Act to be passed; and he wrote *Amelia,* the heroine of which was again drawn from his dear dead Charlotte. This appeared in 1752, and in the same year, such was his energy, he formed a connection with a third newspaper, the *Covent Garden Journal,* which lasted for nine months. His health grew worse and worse, and in 1754, after breaking up "a gang of villains and cutthroats" who had become the terror of London he resigned his office to his half brother John Fielding. It appeared that his only chance of life was to seek a better climate than that of England, and so in June of that year, 1754, he left his native country on the *Queen of Portugal,* Richard Veal, master, for Lisbon. He arrived in August and two months later died. He was buried in the English cemetery.

When I consider Fielding's life, which from inadequate material I have briefly sketched, I am seized with a singular emotion. He was a man. He was fond of the bottle, he was something of a gambler, and he liked women. When people speak of virtue it is generally sex they have in mind, but chastity is only a small part of virtue and perhaps not the chief one. Fielding had strong passions and he had no hesitation in yielding to them. He was capable of loving tenderly. Now love, not affection which is a different thing, is rooted in sex, but there can be sexual desire without love. It is only hypocrisy or ignorance that denies it. Sexual desire is an animal instinct and there is nothing more shameful in it than in thirst or hunger, and no more reason not to satisfy it. If Fielding was dissolute because he enjoyed, somewhat promiscuously, the pleasures of sex, then he was at all events no worse than most men. Like most of us he regretted his sins, but when opportunity occurred, committed them again. He was hot-tempered, but kindhearted, generous, and in a corrupt age honest; an affectionate husband and father; courageous and truthful, and a good friend to his friends, who till his death remained faithful to him. Though tolerant of the faults of others, he hated brutality and double-dealing. He was not puffed up by success and with the help of a chicken and a bottle of champagne bore adversity with fortitude. He took life as it came, with high spirits and good humor, and enjoyed it to the full.

In fact he was very like his own Tom Jones. Now I should like to warn any new reader of Fielding's greatest novel that if he is of a squeamish habit he had better not start on it. It has been well said by Austin Dobson that "he made no pretense to produce models of perfection, but pictures of ordinary humanity, rather perhaps in the rough than in the polished, the natural than the artificial, his desire is to do this with absolute truthfulness, neither extenuating nor disguising defects and shortcomings." In fact he described for the first time in English fiction a real man. Hannah More in her memoirs relates that she never saw Dr. Johnson angry with her but once, and that was when she alluded to some witty passage in *Tom Jones*. "I am shocked to hear you quote from so vicious a book," he said. "I am sorry to hear you have read it: a confession which no modest lady should ever make. I scarcely know a more corrupt work." Now I should say that a modest lady before marriage would do very well to read the book. It will tell her pretty well all she needs to know of the facts of life and a lot about men which cannot fail to be useful to her before entering upon that difficult state. But no one ever has looked upon Dr. Johnson as free from prejudice. He would allow Fielding no literary merit and once described him as a blockhead. When Boswell demurred, he said: "What I mean by his being a blockhead is that he was a barren rascal." "Will you not allow, Sir, that he draws very natural pictures of human life?" answered

Boswell. "Why, Sir, it is of very low life. Richardson used to say that had he not known who Fielding was, he should have believed he was an ostler."

But we are used to low life in fiction now, and there is nothing in *Tom Jones* that the novelists of our own day have not made us familiar with. Prudish critics have sought to explain away as due to the loose morality of the times the incident that has on the whole been looked upon as the most blameworthy in the career of Mr. Jones: Lady Bellaston fell in love with him and found him not unwilling to gratify her desire; he was pretty well penniless at the moment and she was wealthy. She very generously relieved his necessities. Well, it is doubtless a discreditable thing for a man to accept money from a woman, and it is also an unprofitable one, because rich ladies in these circumstances demand a good deal more than their money's worth. Morally it is no more shocking than for a woman to accept money from a man, and it is only a foolishness on the part of common opinion to look upon it as such. Nor should it be forgotten that our own day has found it necessary to invent a term, gigolo, to describe the male who turns his personal attractiveness into a source of profit; so Tom's lack of delicacy, however reprehensible, is not unique.

There is one interesting point in Tom's amorous career that is perhaps worth pointing out. He was honestly, sincerely and deeply in love with the charming Sophia, and yet felt no qualms about indulging in the pleasures of the flesh with any woman who was good-looking and facile. He loved Sophia none the less for these episodes. Fielding was much too sensible to make his hero more continent than is the average sensual man. He knew that we should all be more virtuous if we were as wise at night as we are in the morning.

Tom Jones is well enough constructed and the various incidents follow one another with a happy invention. Fielding was as little concerned with probability as the picaresque novelists who were his predecessors in the genre, and the most unlikely events occur, the most outrageous coincidences bring people together; yet he bustles you along with such gusto that you have hardly time, and in any case little inclination, to protest. The characters are painted in primary colors with a slapdash bravura, and if they somewhat lack subtlety they make

up for it by being very much alive. I'm afraid Mr. Allworthy is a little too good to be true, but here Fielding
has failed as every novelist since has failed who has attempted to depict a perfectly virtuous man. Experience
seems to show that it is impossible not to make him a
trifle stupid. One is impatient with a character who is so
good that he lets the most obvious fakes impose on
him. Ralph Allen of Prior Park is said to have been the
original of Allworthy and it is of him that Pope wrote:

> Let humble Allen, with an awkward shame,
> Do good by stealth and blush to find it fame.

If this is so, and the portrait is accurate, it shows only
that a character taken straight from life is never quite
convincing in a piece of fiction.

Blifil on the other hand has been thought too bad to
be true. Fielding hated deceit and hypocrisy, and his
detestation of Blifil was such that it may be he laid on
his colors with too heavy a hand; but Blifil, a mean,
sneaking, self-seeking, cold-blooded fish, is not an uncommon type. The fear of being found out is the only
thing that restrains him from being a knave. But Blifil's
main fault is that he lacks life, he is a dummy, and I have
asked myself if this is not because of an instinctive feeling on his creator's part that if he had given him a more
active and prominent rôle he would have made him so
powerful and sinister a figure as to upset the balance of
his story.

Tom Jones is written in a very agreeable fashion and
the style is more easy and natural than that of Jane
Austen whose *Pride and Prejudice* was written fifty
years later. The reason for this I take to be that Fielding
modeled himself on Addison and Steele, whereas Jane
Austen was influenced, perhaps unconsciously, by the
pomposity of Dr. Johnson, whom we know she read
with admiration, and by the writers of her own day who
had adopted something of his manner. It has been said,
I forget by whom, that a good style should resemble the
conversation of a cultivated man. That is exactly what
Fielding's style does. He is talking to the reader and telling him the story of *Tom Jones* as he might tell it over
the dinner table with a bottle of wine to a number of
friends. He does not mince his words any more than does

a modern writer. The beautiful and virtuous Sophia was apparently quite used to hearing such words as "whore," "bastard" and "strumpet" and that which, for a reason hard to guess, Fielding writes "b--ch." In fact there were moments when her father, Squire Western, applied them very freely to herself.

But the conversational method of writing a novel, the method by which the author takes you into his confidence, telling you what he feels about the characters and the situations in which they are, has its drawback. The author is always at your elbow and so hinders your immediate communication with the persons of his story. He is apt to irritate you sometimes by moralizing, and once he starts to digress is apt to be tedious. You do not want to hear what he has to say about this, that and the other; you want him to get on with the story. Fielding's digressions are nearly always sensible or amusing, and their only fault is that one could well do without them. But they are brief, and he has the grace to apologize for them.

But he went further than that. He prefaced each of the books into which *Tom Jones* is divided with an essay. Some critics have greatly admired them and have looked upon them as adding to the excellence of the book. I can only suppose that is because they were not interested in the novel as a novel. An essayist takes a subject and discusses it. If his subject is new to you, he may tell you something that you didn't know before, but new subjects are hard to find and in general he expects to interest you by his own attitude and the characteristic way he regards things. That is to say he expects to interest you in himself. But that is the last thing you are prepared to do when you read a novel. You don't care a row of pins about the author; he is there to tell you a story and introduce to you a group of characters. Because it has been my business I have read the essays with which Fielding introduced his various books, but, although I would not deny their merit, I have read them with impatience. The reader of a novel should want to know what happens next to the characters in whom the author has interested him and if he doesn't there is no reason for him to read the novel at all. For the novel, I can never repeat too often, is not to be looked upon as a medium of instruction or edification, but as a source of intelligent entertainment.

On reading over these pages I find myself fearing that
I have given the reader of this introduction the impression that *Tom Jones* is a rough, coarse book, dealing
with adventurers and loose women, and vulgar. That
would be a very false impression. Fielding knew life too
well to take people at their face value and his experience
had shown him that it is not in human nature to be entirely disinterested. Complete unselfishness is beautiful,
but it is not of this world and it is ingenuous to expect it.
But in Sophia Western he has drawn a charming and
tender portrait of as delightful a young woman as has
ever enchanted a reader of fiction. She is simple, but not
silly, virtuous but no prude; she has character, determination and courage; she has a loving heart and she is
beautiful. It is touching to know that in creating her
Fielding was remembering his own beloved (and, I am
afraid, long-suffering) wife.

I do not think I can end this introduction better than
by quoting the words of that wise critic George Saints-
bury:

"Tom Jones is an epic of life—not indeed of the highest, the rarest, the most impassioned of life's scenes and
phases, but of the healthy average life of the average natural man; not faultless nor perfect by any means, but
human and actual as no one else but Shakespeare has
shown him in the mimic world."

JANE AUSTEN
and
PRIDE AND PREJUDICE

THE EVENTS of Jane Austen's life can be told very briefly. The Austens were an old family whose fortunes, like those of many of the greatest families in England, had been founded on the wool trade, which was at one time the country's staple industry; having made money, again like others of more importance, they bought land and so in time joined the ranks of the country gentry. Jane was born in 1775 at Steventon, a village in Hampshire, of which her father, the Rev. George Austen, was rector. She was the youngest of seven children. When she was sixteen her father resigned his living, and with his wife and his two girls, Cassandra and Jane, for his sons were already out in the world, moved to Bath. He died in 1805, and his widow and daughters settled at Southampton. Not long afterwards one of Jane's brothers inherited estates in Kent and in Hampshire, and offered his mother a cottage on either of them. She chose to go to Chawton in Hampshire—this was in 1809—and there, with occasional visits to friends and relations, Jane remained till illness obliged her to go to Winchester in order to put herself in the hands of better doctors than could be found in a village, and there she died in 1817. She was buried in the cathedral.

She is said to have been in person very attractive; "her figure was rather tall and slender, her step light and firm, and her whole appearance expressive of health and animation. In complexion she was a clear brunette with a rich color; she had full round cheeks with mouth and nose small and well-formed, bright hazel eyes, and brown hair forming natural curls close round her face." The only portrait of her I have seen shows a fat-faced young woman with undistinguished features, large round eyes and an obtrusive bust; but it may be that the artist did her less than justice. She had a rare and racy sense of humor, and since she says that her conversation was exactly like her letters, and her letters are full of witty, ironical and malicious remarks, it is impossible to doubt that her conversation was brilliant.

Most of the letters that have remained were written to her sister Cassandra. She was greatly attached to her. As girls and women they were constantly together, and indeed shared the same bedroom till Jane's death. When Cassandra was sent to school Jane went with her because, though too young to profit by such instruction as the seminary for young ladies provided, she would have been wretched without her. "If Cassandra were going to have her head cut off," said her mother, "Jane would insist on sharing her fate." Cassandra was handsomer than Jane, of a colder and calmer disposition, less demonstrative and of a less sunny nature; she had "the merit of always having her temper under command, but Jane had the happiness of a temper that never required to be commanded." Many of Jane Austen's warmest admirers have found her letters disappointing, and have thought they showed that she was cold and unfeeling and that her interests were trivial. I am surprised. They are very natural. Jane Austen never imagined that anyone but Cassandra would read them, and she told her exactly the sort of things she knew would interest her. She told her what people were wearing and how much she had paid for the flowered muslin she had bought, what acquaintances she had made, what old friends she had met and the gossip she had heard.

Of late years several collections of letters by eminent authors have been published, and for my part, when I read them, I am now and then disposed to suspect that the writers had at the back of their minds the notion that one day they might find their way into print. They give me not seldom the impression that they might have been used just as they were in the columns of a literary journal. In order not to annoy the devotees of the recently deceased I will not mention their names, but Dickens has been dead a long time and it is possible to say what one likes of him without offense. Whenever he went on a journey he wrote long letters to his friends in which he described eloquently the sights he had seen and which, as his biographer justly observes, might well have been printed without the alteration of a single word. People were more patient in those days: still one would have thought it a disappointment to receive a letter from a friend who gave you word pictures of mountains and monuments when you wanted to know whether he had come across anyone interesting, what parties he had been to and whether he had been able to get you the books or ties or handkerchiefs you had asked him to bring back.

Jane Austen hardly ever wrote a letter that had not a smile or a laugh in it, and for the delectation of the reader I will give a few examples of her manner. I can only regret that I have not space for more.

"Single women have a dreadful propensity for being poor, which is one very strong argument in favor of matrimony."

"Only think of Mrs. Holder being dead! Poor woman, she has done the only thing in the world she could possibly do to make one cease to abuse her."

"Mrs. Hall, of Sherborne, was brought to bed yesterday of a dead child, some weeks before she expected, owing to a fright. I suppose she happened unawares to look at her husband."

"The death of Mrs. W. K. we had seen. I had no idea that anybody liked her, and therefore felt nothing for any survivor, but I am now feeling away on her husband's account, and think he had better marry Miss Sharpe."

"I respect Mrs. Chamberlayne for doing her hair well, but cannot feel a more tender sentiment. Miss Langley is like any other short girl with a broad nose and wide mouth, fashionable dress and exposed bosom. Admiral Stanhope is a gentlemanlike man, but then his legs are too short and his tail too long."

Jane Austen was fond of dancing. Here are a few comments connected with balls she went to.

"There were only twelve dances, of which I danced nine, and was merely prevented from dancing the rest by want of a partner."

"There was one gentleman, an officer of the Cheshire, a very good-looking young man, who, I was told, wanted very much to be introduced to me; but as he did not want it quite enough to take much trouble in effecting it, we never could bring it about."

"There were few beauties, and such as there were,

were not very handsome. Miss Iremonger did not look well and Mrs. Blunt was the only one much admired. She appeared exactly as she did in September, with the same broad face, diamond bandeau, white shoes, pink husband and fat neck."

"Charles Powlett gave a dance on Thursday to the great disturbance of all his neighbours, of course, who you know take a most lively interest in the state of his finances, and live in hopes of his being soon ruined. His wife is discovered to be everything that the neighbourhood would wish her to be, silly and cross as well as extravagant."

"Mrs. Richard Harvey is going to be married, but as it is a great secret, and only known to half the neighbourhood, you must not mention it."

"Dr. Hall is in such very deep mourning that either his mother, his wife or himself must be dead."

When Miss Austen was living with her mother at Southampton they paid a call and this is what she wrote to Cassandra:

"We found only Mrs. Lance at home, and whether she boasts any offspring besides a grand pianoforte did not appear. . . . They live in a handsome style and are rich, and she seems to like to be rich; we gave her to understand that we were far from being so; she will soon feel therefore that we are not worth her acquaintance."

A relation of Jane's seems to have given occasion to gossip owing to the behavior of a certain Dr. Mant, behavior such that his wife retired to her mother's, whereupon Jane wrote: "But as Dr. M. is a clergyman their attachment, however immoral, has a decorous air."

She had a sharp tongue and a prodigious sense of humor. She liked to laugh and she liked to make others laugh. It is asking too much of the humorist to expect him —or her—to keep a good thing to himself when he thinks of it. And, heaven knows, it is hard to be funny without being sometimes a trifle malicious. There is not much kick in the milk of human kindness. Jane had a keen appreciation of the absurdity of others, their pretentiousness, their affectations and their insincerities; and it is to her credit that they amused rather than annoyed her. She was too amiable to say things to people that would pain them, but she certainly saw no harm in amusing herself at their expense with Cassandra. I find no ill nature in even the most biting and witty of her remarks; her humor was based, as humor should be, on accurate observation and frankness.

It has been remarked that though she lived through some of the most stirring events of the world's history, the French Revolution, the Terror, the rise and fall of Napoleon, she made no reference to them in her novels. She has on this account been blamed for an undue detachment. It should be remembered that in her day it was not polite for women to occupy themselves with politics, that was a matter for men to deal with; they did not even read the newspapers; but there is no reason to suppose that because she did not write about these events she was not affected by them. She was fond of her family, two of her brothers were in the navy, often enough in danger, and her letters show that they were much on her mind. But did she not show her good sense in not writing about such matters? She was too modest ever to suppose that her novels would be read long after her death, but if that had been her aim she could not have acted more wisely than she did in avoiding to deal with affairs which from the literary standpoint were of passing interest. Already the novels concerned with the Great War that have been written in the last few years are as dead as mutton. They were as ephemeral as the newspapers that day by day told us what was happening.

There is a passage in Austen Leigh's *Life* from which, by the exercise of a little imagination, one can get an idea of the sort of existence Miss Austen must have led during those long quiet years in the country. "It may be asserted as a general truth, that less was left to the charge and discretion of servants, and more was done, or superintended by the masters and mistresses. With regard to the mistresses, it is, I believe, generally understood that . . . they took a personal part in the higher branches of cookery, as well as in the concoction of home-made wines, and distilling of herbs for domestic medicines. . . . Ladies did not disdain to spin the thread out of which the household linen was woven. Some ladies liked to wash with their own hands their choice china after breakfast or tea." Miss Austen took a healthy interest in gowns, bonnets and scarves; and she was a fine needlewoman, both plain and ornamental. She very properly liked young men to be good-looking and had no objection to flirting with them. She loved not only dancing, but theatricals, card games and other more simple amusements. She was "successful in everything that she attempted with her fingers. None of us could throw spillikins in so perfect a circle, or take them off with so steady a hand. Her performances with a cup and ball were marvellous. The one used at Chawton was an easy one, and she has been known to catch it on the point an hundred times in succession, till her hand was weary." It is not surprising to learn that she was a favorite with children; they liked her playful ways with them and her long circumstantial stories.

No one could describe Jane Austen as a bluestocking (a type with which she had no sympathy) but it is plain that she was a cultivated woman. R. W. Chapman, the great authority on her novels, made a list of the books she is known to have read and it is an imposing one. Of course she read novels, Fanny Burney's, Marie Edgeworth's and Mrs. Radcliffe's (*The Mysteries of Udolpho*); and she read novels translated from the French and German (among others Goethe's *Sorrows of Werther*); and whatever others she could get from the circulating library at Bath and Southampton. She knew her Shakespeare well, and among the moderns she read Scott and Byron, but her favorite poet seems to have been Cowper. It is not hard to see why his cool, elegant and sensible verse appealed to her. She read Dr. Johnson and Boswell, a good deal of history and not a few sermons.

This brings me to what is obviously the most important thing about her, the books she wrote. She began writing at a very early age. When she was dying at Winchester she sent a niece who had taken to writing a message to the effect that if she would take her advice she would cease doing so till she was sixteen, and that she had herself often wished that she had read more and written less in the corresponding years (twelve to sixteen) of her own life. At that time it was thought far from ladylike for a woman to write books. Monk Lewis wrote: "I have an aversion, a pity and contempt for all female scribblers. The needle, not the pen, is the instrument they should handle, and the only one they ever use dexterously." The novel was a form held in low esteem, and Jane Austen was herself not a little shocked that Sir Walter Scott, a poet, should write fiction. She was "careful that her occupation should not be suspected by servants, or visitors, or any person beyond her family party. She wrote upon small sheets of paper which could easily be put away, or covered with a piece of blotting paper. There was between the front door and the offices, a swing door which creaked when it was opened; but she objected to having this little inconvenience remedied, because it gave her notice when anyone was coming." Her eldest brother, James, never even told his son, then a boy at school, that the books he read with delight were by his Aunt Jane; and her brother Henry in his memoir states: "No accumulation of fame would have induced her, had she lived, to affix her name to any productions of her pen." So her first book to be published, *Sense and Sensibility,* was described on the title page as "by a Lady."

It was not the first she wrote. That was the novel called *First Impressions.* Her brother, George Austen, wrote to a publisher offering for publication, at the author's expense or otherwise, a "manuscript novel, comprising three volumes; about the length of Miss Burney's *Evelina.*" The offer was refused by return of post. *First Impressions* was begun during the winter of 1796 and finished in August 1797; it is generally supposed to have been substantially the same book as sixteen years later was issued as *Pride and Prejudice.* Then, in quick succession, she wrote *Sense and Sensibility* and *Northanger Abbey,* but had no better luck with them, though after five years a Mr. Richard Crosby bought the latter, then called *Susan,* for £10. He never published it and eventually sold it back for what he had paid. Since Miss Austen's novels had been published anonymously he had no notion that the book he parted with for so small a sum was by the successful and popular author of *Pride and Prejudice.*

She seems to have written nothing but a fragment called *The Watsons* between 1798 when she finished *Northanger Abbey* and 1809. It is a long interval for a writer of such gifts to wait, and it has been suggested that her silence was due to a love affair that occupied her to the exclusion of other interests. But this is mere surmise. She was young in 1798—twenty-four—and it is likely enough that she fell in love more than once, but she was hard to please, and it is equally likely that she fell out again without any great perturbation of spirit. The most probable explanation of her long silence is that she was discouraged by her inability to find a publisher. Her close relations, to whom she read them, were charmed with them, but she was as sensible as she was modest, and she may well have concluded that their appeal was only to persons who were fond of her and had, it may be, a shrewd idea who the models of her characters were.

Anyhow in 1809, in which year she settled with her mother and sister in the quiet of Chawton, she set about revising her old manuscripts, and in 1811 *Sense and Sensibility* at last appeared. By then it was no longer outrageous for a woman to write. Professor Spurgeon in a lecture on Jane Austen delivered to the Royal Society of Literature quotes a preface to *Original Letters from India* by Eliza Fay. This lady had been urged to publish them in 1782, but public opinion was so averse "to female authorship" that she declined. But writing in 1816, she said: "Since then a considerable change has gradually taken place in public sentiment, and its development; we have now not only as in former days a number of women who do honour to their sex as literary characters, but many unpretending females, who fearless of the critical perils that once attended the voyage, venture to launch their little barks on the vast ocean through which amusement or instruction is conveyed to a reading public."

Pride and Prejudice was published in 1813. Jane Austen sold the copyright for £10.

Besides the three novels already mentioned she wrote three more, *Mansfield Park, Emma* and *Persuasion*. On these few books her fame rests, and her fame is secure. She had to wait a long time to get a book published, but she no sooner did than her charming gifts were recognized. Since then the most eminent persons have agreed to praise her. I will only quote what Sir Walter Scott had to say; it is characteristically generous: "That young lady had a talent for describing the involvements, feelings and characters of ordinary life which is to me the most wonderful I have ever met with. The big bow-wow I can do myself like anyone going; but the exquisite touch which renders commonplace things and characters interesting from the truth of the description and the sentiment is denied to me."

It is odd that Scott should have omitted to make mention of the young lady's most precious talent: her observation was searching and her sentiment edifying, but it was her humor that gave point to her observation and a kind of prim liveliness to her sentiment. Her range was narrow. She wrote very much the same sort of story in all her books, and there is no great variety in her characters. They are very much the same persons seen from a somewhat different point of view. She had common sense in a high degree, and no one knew better than she her limitations. Her experience of life was confined to a small circle of provincial society, and that is what she was content to deal with.

She wrote only of what she knew; and it has been noticed that she never attempted to reproduce a conversation of men when by themselves, which in the nature of things she could never have heard.

She shared the opinions common in her day and, so far as one can tell from her books and letters, was quite satisfied with the conditions that prevailed. She had no doubt that social distinctions were important, and she found it natural that there should be rich and poor. A gentleman's younger son was properly provided for by taking orders and being given a fat family living; young men obtained advancement in the service of the King by the influence of powerful relations; a woman's business was to marry, for love certainly, but in satisfactory financial circumstances. All this was in the order of things, and there is no sign that Miss Austen saw anything objectionable in it. Her family was connected with the clergy and the landed gentry, and her novels are concerned with no other class.

It is difficult to decide which is the best of them because they are all so good, and each one has its devoted and even fanatic, admirers. Macaulay thought *Mansfield Park* her greatest achievement; other critics, equally illustrious, have preferred *Emma;* Disraeli read *Pride and Prejudice* seventeen times; today many look upon *Persuasion* as her most exquisite and finished work. The great mass of readers, I believe, has accepted *Pride and Prejudice* as her masterpiece, and in such a case I think it well to accept their judgment. What makes a classic is not that it is praised by critics, expounded by professors and studied in college classes, but that the great mass of readers, generation after generation, have found pleasure and spiritual profit in reading it.

My own opinion, for what it is worth, is that *Pride and Prejudice* is on the whole the most satisfactory of all the novels. *Emma* offends me by the snobbishness of the heroine; she is really too patronizing to the persons she looks upon as her social inferiors, and I can take no particular interest in the love affair of Frank Churchill and Jane Fairfax. It is the only one of Miss Austen's novels that I find long-winded. In *Mansfield Park* the hero and heroine, Fanny and Edmund, are intolerable prigs, and all my sympathies go out to the unscrupulous, sprightly and charming Henry and Mary Crawford. *Persuasion* has a rare charm, and except for the incident on the Cobb at Lyme Regis I should be forced to look upon it as the most perfect of the six. Jane Austen had no great gift for inventing incident of an unusual character, and this one seems to me a very clumsy contrivance. Louisa Musgrove runs up some steep steps, and is "jumped down" by her admirer Captain Wentworth. He misses her, she falls on her head and is stunned. If he was going to give her his hands, as we are told he had been in the habit of doing in "jumping her off" a stile, she could not have been more than six feet up, and as she was jumping down it is impossible that she should have fallen on her head. In any case she would have fallen against the stalwart sailor, and though perhaps shaken and frightened could hardly have hurt herself. Anyhow, she was unconscious, and the fuss that was made is unbelievable. Everybody loses his head. Captain Wentworth, who has seen action and made a fortune out of prize money, is paralyzed with horror. The immediately subsequent behavior of all concerned is so idiotic that I find it hard to believe that Miss Austen, who was able to take the illnesses and deaths of her friends and relations with considerable fortitude, did not look upon it as uncommonly foolish.

Professor Garrod, a learned and witty critic, has said that Jane Austen was incapable of writing a story, by which, he explains, he means a sequence of happenings, either romantic or uncommon. But that is not what Jane Austen had a talent for, and not what she tried to do. She had too much common sense and too sprightly a humor to be romantic, and she was not interested in the uncommon, but in the common. She made it uncommon by the keenness of her observation, her irony and her playful wit. By a story most of us mean a connected and coherent narrative with a beginning, a middle and an end. *Pride and Prejudice* begins in the right place, with the arrival on the scene of the two young men whose love for Elizabeth Bennet and her sister Jane is the main theme of the novel, and it ends in the right place with their marriage. It is the traditional happy ending. This sort of ending has excited the scorn of the sophisticated, and of course it is true that many, perhaps most, marriages are not happy, and further, that marriage concludes nothing; it is merely an entry upon another order of experience. Many authors have in consequence started their novels with marriage and dealt with its outcome. It is their right. But I have a notion that there is something to be said for the simple people who look upon marriage as a satisfactory conclusion to a work of fiction. I think they do so because they have a deep, instinctive feeling that by mating, a man and a woman have fulfilled their biological function; the interest which it is natural to feel in the steps that have led to this consummation, the birth of love, the obstacles, the misunderstandings, the avowals, now yields to its result, their issue, which is the generation that will succeed them. To nature each couple is but a link in a chain, and the only importance of the link is that another link may be added to it. This is the novelist's justification for the happy ending. In Jane Austen's books the reader's satisfaction is considerably enhanced by the knowledge that the bridegroom has a substantial income from real estate and will take his bride to a fine house, surrounded by a park, and furnished throughout with expensive and elegant furniture.

Pride and Prejudice seems to me a very well-constructed book. The incidents follow one another naturally, and one's sense of probability is nowhere outraged. It is, perhaps, odd that Elizabeth and Jane should be so well-bred and well-behaved, whereas their mother and three younger sisters should be so ordinary; but that this should be so was essential to the story Miss Austen had to tell. I have allowed myself to wonder why she did not avoid this stumblingblock by making Elizabeth and Jane the daughters of a first marriage of Mr. Bennet and making the Mrs. Bennet of the novel his second wife and the mother of the three younger daughters. Jane Austen liked Elizabeth best of all her heroines. "I must confess," she wrote, "that I think her as delightful a creature as ever appeared in print." If, as some have thought, she was herself the original for her portrait of Elizabeth—and she has certainly given her her own gaiety, high spirit and courage, wit and readiness, good sense and right feeling—it is perhaps not rash to suppose that when she drew the placid, kindly and beautiful Jane Bennet she had in mind her sister Cassandra. Darcy has been generally regarded as a fearful cad. His first offense was his refusal to dance with people he didn't know and didn't want to know at a public ball to which he had gone with a party. Not a very heinous one. It is true that when he proposes to Elizabeth it is with an unpardonable insolence, but pride, pride of birth and wealth, was the predominant trait of his character, and without it there would have been no story to tell. The manner of his proposal, moreover, gave Jane Austen opportunity for the most dramatic scene in the book; it is conceivable that with the experience she gained later she might have been able to indicate Darcy's feelings in such a way as to antagonize Elizabeth without putting into his mouth speeches so improbable as to shock the reader. There is perhaps some exaggeration in the drawing of Lady Catherine and Mr. Collins, but to my mind little more than comedy allows. Comedy sees life in a light more sparkling, but colder than that of common day, and a touch of exaggeration, that is of farce, is often no disadvantage. A discreet admixture of farce, like a sprinkle of sugar on strawberries, may well make comedy more palatable. With regard to Lady Catherine one must remember that in Jane Austen's day rank gave its possessors a sense of immense superiority over persons of inferior station, and not only expected to be treated by them with the utmost deference, but were. If Lady Catherine looked upon Elizabeth as so much white trash, let us not forget that Elizabeth looked upon her Aunt Phillips, because she was the wife of an attorney, as very little better. In my own youth, a hundred years after Jane Austen wrote, I knew great ladies whose sense of importance, though not quite so blatant, was not far removed from Lady Catherine's. And as for Mr. Collins, who has not known even today men with that combination of pomposity and sycophancy?

No one has ever looked upon Jane Austen as a great stylist. Her spelling was peculiar and her grammar often shaky, but she had a good ear. I think the influence of Dr. Johnson can be discerned in the structure of her sentences. She is apt to use the word of Latin origin rather than the plain English one, the abstract rather than the concrete. It gives her phrase a slight formality which is far from unpleasant; indeed it often adds point to a witty remark and a demure savor to a malicious one. Her dialogue is probably as natural as dialogue can ever be. To set down on paper speech as it is spoken would be very tedious, and some arrangement of it is necessary. Since so many of the speeches are worded exactly as they would be today we must suppose that at the end of the eighteenth century young girls in conversation did express themselves in a manner which would now seem stilted. Jane Bennett, speaking of her lover's sisters, remarks: "They were certainly no friends to his acquaintance with me, which I cannot wonder at, since he might have chosen so much more advantageously in many respects." I am willing to believe that this is just how she put it, but I admit, it requires an effort.

I have said nothing yet of what to my mind is the greatest merit of this charming book: it is wonderfully readable—more readable than some greater and more famous novels. As Scott said, Miss Austen deals with commonplace things, the involvements, feelings and characters of ordinary life; nothing very much happens and yet when you reach the bottom of a page you eagerly turn it in order to know what will happen next; nothing very much does and again you turn the page with the same eagerness.

After I had finished this essay I happened one evening to be sitting at dinner next to a lady who was related to a descendant of Jane Austen's brother. This brother, the

reader will remember, was left large properties in Kent
and Hampshire by a cousin, and by the testator's will had
to adopt the name of Knight. He had daughters, one of
whom, Fanny, was Jane Austen's favorite niece. She
grew up, and by her marriage became Lady Knatchbull.
Our conversation at dinner turned upon Jane Austen,
and my neighbor told me that this relation of hers had an
unpublished letter from Lady Knatchbull to her younger
sister, Mrs. Rice, in which she spoke of her famous aunt.
I was of course all eagerness to see it, and shortly afterwards the kind lady sent me a copy of it. It was so surprising, so characteristic of the period in which it was
written, and in its own way so diverting that I felt it
should be published. By permission of Lord Brabourne,
a direct descendant of Lady Knatchbull, I am now enabled to do so. The italics mark the words she underlined.

It may be surmised from the way the letter begins that
Mrs. Rice was uneasy about some things she had heard
that reflected on her Aunt Jane's gentility, and had written to inquire if they were by any frightful chance true.
Lady Knatchbull replied as follows:

Yes my love it is very true that Aunt Jane from various
circumstances was not so *refined* as she ought to have been
from her *talent*, & if she had lived 50 years later she would
have been in many respects more suitable to our more refined tastes. They were not rich & the people around with
whom they chiefly mixed, were not at all high bred, or in
short anything more than *mediocre* & *they* of course tho'
superior in *mental powers & cultivation* were on the same
level as far as *refinement* goes—but I think in later life their
intercourse with Mrs. Knight (who was very fond of & kind
to them) improved them both & Aunt Jane was too clever
not to put aside all possible signs of 'common-ness' (if such
an expression is allowable) & teach herself to be more refined,
at least in intercourse with people in general. Both the
Aunts (Cassandra & Jane) were brought up in the most complete ignorance of the World & its ways (I mean as to fashion
etc) & if it had not been for Papa's marriage which brought
them into Kent, & the kindness of Mrs. Knight, who used
often to have one or the other of the sisters staying with her,
they would have been, tho' not less clever and agreeable in
themselves, very much below par as to good Society and its
ways. If you hate all this I beg yr. pardon, but I felt it at my

pen's end & it chose to come along & speak the truth. It is now nearly dressing time . . .

   . . . I am ever beloved Sister yours most affec.

F.C.K.

It just shows that you may make a great stir in the world and yet sadly fail to impress the members of your own family.

STENDHAL
and
THE RED AND THE BLACK

I HAVE FOUND it impossible in the few pages at my disposal to give a reasonably lucid account of the life of Henri Beyle, who is known to fame as Stendhal. It would need a book to tell his story, and to make it comprehensible I should have to go into the social and political history of the time. Fortunately the book has been written, and if the reader of *The Red and the Black* is sufficiently interested to want to know more about its author than I have space to tell him he cannot do better than read the lively and well-documented life that Mr. Matthew Josephson has recently published under the title: *Stendhal or The Pursuit of Happiness.* I can thus content myself with giving the bare facts of Stendhal's biography.

He was born at Grenoble in 1783, the son of an attorney, a man of property and of some consequence. His mother, the daughter of the principal doctor in the city, died when he was seven.

In 1789 the French Revolution broke out. In 1792 Louis XVI and Marie Antoinette were executed.

Stendhal has described at length his life as child and boy, and it is interesting to study because during this period he conceived prejudices which he maintained to his life's end. On the death of his mother, whom he loved, as he himself says, with a lover's love, he was left to the care of his father and his mother's sister. His father was a grave, conscientious man; his aunt strict and devout. He hated them. Though belonging to the middle class they had aristocratic leanings, and the revolution filled them with dismay. Stendhal claims that his childhood was miserable, but it does not appear from his own account that he had much to complain of. He was clever, argumentative and very much of a handful.

When the Terror reached Grenoble Stendhal's father was placed on the list of suspects; he thought he owed this to a rival lawyer, named Amar, who wanted his practice: "But Amar," said the smart little boy, "has put you on the list of those suspected of not loving the republic, and it is certain that you do not love it." True, of course, but not very pleasant for a middle-aged gentleman who is in danger of losing his head to hear from his only son. Stendhal accused his father of a horrid stinginess, but he seems always to have been able to wheedle money out of him when he wanted it. He was forbidden to read certain books, but he read them all the same. This is what has occurred to thousands upon thousands of children all the world over since books were first printed. His chief complaint was that he was not permitted to mix freely with other children, but his life could not have been so solitary as he makes out, since he had two sisters, and other little boys shared his lessons with the Jesuit priest who was his tutor. He was in fact brought up as children in the well-to-do middle class were brought up at the time. Like all children he looked upon ordinary restraints as the exercise of outrageous tyranny, and when he was obliged to learn his lessons, when he was not allowed to do exactly as he liked, regarded himself as treated with monstrous cruelty.

In this he was like most children, but most children, when they grow up, forget their grievances. Stendhal was unusual in that at fifty-three he harbored his old resentments. Because he hated his Jesuit tutor he became violently anti-clerical, and to the end of his life could never bring himself to believe that a religious person might be sincere. Because his father and his aunt were devoted royalists he became ardently republican. But when one evening, being then eleven years old, he slipped out of the house to go to a revolutionary meeting he had something of a shock. He found the proletariat dirty and smelly, vulgar and ill-spoken. "In short, I was then as I am today," he wrote. "I love the people, I hate their oppressors, but it would be a perpetual torture for me to live with the people. . . . I had, and I have still, the most aristocratic tastes; I would do everything for the happiness of the people, but I would sooner, I believe, pass two weeks every month in prison than live

with shopkeepers." One cannot but smile when one re-
flects how like this attitude is to that of the bright young
rebels whom one meets now and then in the drawing-
rooms of the rich.

Stendhal was sixteen when he first went to Paris. His
father gave him an introduction to a connection of his, a
Monsieur Daru, whose two sons were in the War Office.
Pierre, the elder, was in charge of a department, and
after some time engaged his young cousin as one of his
many secretaries. Napoleon set out on his second cam-
paign in Italy, the brothers Daru followed him, and shortly afterwards Stendhal joined them at Milan. After some
months on the clerical staff Pierre Daru got him a commission in a regiment of dragoons, but, enjoying the gaieties of Milan as he did, he made no attempt to join his
regiment and, taking advantage of Daru's absence, he
wheedled a certain General Michaud into making him
his A.D.C. When Pierre Daru came back he ordered
Stendhal to join his regiment, but this on one pretext and
another he avoided doing for six months, and when at
last he did, found himself so bored that on a plea of illness he got leave of absence to go home and resigned his
commission. He saw no action, but this did not prevent
him from boasting in after years of his prowess as a com-
batant; and indeed, in 1804, when he was looking for a
job he wrote a testimonial himself (which General
Michaud signed) in which he certified to his gallantry in
various battles which it has been proved he could not
possibly have fought in.

He went to live in Paris on a small, but sufficient allowance from his father. He had two objects in view.
One was to become the greatest dramatic poet of the
age. He studied a manual of playwriting and went to the
theater nearly every day. He noted in his diary the
plays he had seen and what he thought of them. Over
and over again one finds him remarking how he could
work up a play he had just seen into one of his own. He
seems to have had no ideas, and he was certainly no
poet. His other object was to become a great lover. But
for this nature had ill equipped him; he was somewhat
undersized, an ugly, plump young man with a big body
and short legs, a large head and a mass of black hair;
his mouth was thin, his nose thick and prominent; but
his eyes were brown and eager, his feet and his hands

small and his skin as delicate as a woman's. He was proud to declare that to hold a sword raised blisters on his hand. He was besides shy and awkward. Through his cousin Martial Daru, Pierre's younger brother, he was able to frequent the salons of some of the ladies whose husbands the revolution had enriched, but he was sadly tongue-tied in company. He could think of clever things to say, but could never summon up the courage to say them. It cramped his style. He was angrily conscious of his provincial accent, and it may be that it was to cure himself of this that he entered a dramatic school. Here he met an actress, Mélanie Guilbert by name, two or three years older than himself, and after some hesitation decided to fall in love with her. He hesitated partly because he was not sure whether she had a greatness of soul equal to his own and partly because he suspected that she was suffering from a veneral disease. Having presumably satisfied himself on both points, he followed her to Marseilles, where she had an engagement and where for some months he worked at a wholesale grocer's. He came to the conclusion that she was not, either spiritually or intellectually, the woman he had thought, and it was a relief to him when want of money obliged her to return to Paris.

I have no space to deal with the various love affairs that occupied Stendhal's life, but only with the two or three that throw light on his character. He was highly sex-conscious, but not particularly sexual; indeed until some very frank letters were discovered from one of his later mistresses it was suspected that he was sexually frigid. His passions were cerebral, and to possess a woman was chiefly a satisfaction to his vanity. Notwithstanding his high-flown phrases, there is no sign that he was capable of tenderness. He admits frankly enough that most of his love affairs were unfortunate, and it is not hard to see why. He was faint-hearted. When in Italy he asked a brother officer how to go about it to win a woman's "favors," and solemnly wrote down the advice he received. He laid siege to women by rule, just as he had tried to write plays by rule; and he was affronted when he discovered that they thought him ridiculous, and surprised when they discerned his insincerity. Clever as he was, it seems never to have occurred to him that the language a woman understands is the language of the heart, and that the language of reason leaves her cold. He thought he could achieve by stratagem and chicanery what can only be achieved by feeling.

Stendhal went back to Paris some months after Mélanie Guilbert left him, and through the influence of Pierre Daru obtained a post in the commissariat. He was posted to Brunswick. He abandoned the idea of being a great dramatist, and decided to make a career for himself in the bureaucracy. He saw himself as a baron of the Empire, a knight of the Legion of Honour and finally as Préfet of a department with a princely salary. Ardent republican though he was, and looking upon Napoleon as a tyrant who had robbed France of her liberty, he wrote to his father asking him to buy him a title. He added the *de* to his name and called himself Henri de Beyle. But he was a competent and resourceful administrator; and in 1810, having gained promotion, he found himself back in Paris with an office in a superb suite in the Palace of the Invalides. He acquired a cabriolet, with a pair of horses, a coachman and a man servant. He took a little chorus girl to live with him, but that did not suffice; he felt that he owed it to himself to have a mistress he could love and whose position would add to his prestige. He decided that Alexandrine Daru would fill the bill. She was a handsome woman, the wife of Pierre Daru, now a count, but many years younger than her husband, by whom she had had four children. There is no sign that Stendhal gave a thought to the kindness and long-suffering tolerance with which his cousin Pierre had treated him, nor that, since he owed his advancement to him and his career depended on his good graces, it was neither politic nor elegant to seduce his wife. Gratitude was a virtue unknown to him.

He set about the attack with his armory of amorous devices, but the unfortunate diffidence of which he could not rid himself still hampered him. He was by turns sprightly and sad, flirtatious and cold, ardent and indifferent: nothing seemed to be of any use, and he could not make out whether the Countess loved him or not. It was a mortification to him to suspect that because of his bashfulness she laughed at him behind his back. At length he went to an old friend and having told him his troubles, asked him what tactics to pursue. They talked the matter over. The friend asked questions, Stendhal answered them, and the friend wrote them down. Here, as summarized by Matthew Josephson, are the answers to the question: "What are the advantages of seducing Madame de B.?" (Madame de B. was what they called Countess Daru.) "They are as follows: He would be following the inclinations of his character; he would win great social advantages; he would pursue further his study of human passions; he would satisfy honour and pride." A footnote to the document was written by Stendhal: "The best advice. Attack! Attack! Attack!" It was good advice, but not easy to follow when you are cursed with an insurmountable timidity. Some weeks later he was invited to stay at Bècheville, the Darus' country house, and on the second morning, after a sleepless night, resolved to take the plunge, he put on his best striped pants. Countess Daru complimented him on them. They walked in the garden, while a friend of hers, with her mother and the children, followed twenty yards behind. They strolled up and down, and Stendhal, trembling but determined, fixed upon a certain point, which he called A from the point B where they then were, and swore that if when they reached it he did not speak out he would kill himself. He spoke, he seized her hand and tried to kiss it. He told her that he had loved her for eighteen months, had done his best to conceal it, and even tried not to see her, but could bear his agony no longer. She replied, not unkindly, that she had no feeling for him greater than friendship and no wish to be unfaithful to her husband. She called the rest of the party to join them. Stendhal had lost what he called the Battle of Bècheville. It may be surmised that his vanity rather than his heart was wounded.

Two months later, still smarting from his disappointment, he applied for leave of absence and went to Milan, which he had fallen in love with on his first visit to Italy. There, ten years before, he had been attracted by a certain Gina Pietragrua, who was the mistress of a brother officer of his; but he was then a penniless sub-lieutenant and she had paid little attention to him. He thought he would look her up. Her father kept a shop, and when quite young she had married a government clerk. By this time she was thirty-four with a son of sixteen. On seeing her again, Stendhal found her "a tall and superb woman. She still had something of the majestic in her eyes, expression, brow and nose. I found her (he adds) cleverer, with more majesty and less of that full grace of voluptuousness." She was certainly clever enough on her husband's small salary to have an apartment in Milan, a house in the country, servants, a box at the Scala and a carriage.

Stendhal was highly conscious of his ugliness, and to overcome it made a point of dressing with elegance and fashion. He had always been plump, but by now with good living he was grown portly; however, he had money in his pocket and fine clothes to his back. He had evidently more chance of pleasing the majestic lady than when he was a poverty-stricken dragoon. He decided to amuse himself with her during his short stay in Milan, but she was not so facile as he had expected. She led him a dance, and it was not till the eve of his departure for Rome that she consented to receive him in her apartment early one morning. One would have thought it an unpropitious hour for love. That day he wrote in his diary: "On the 21st September at half past eleven, I won the victory I had so long desired." He also wrote the date on his suspenders. He had worn the same striped pants as on the day of his declaration to Countess Daru.

In 1812 Stendhal, having with difficulty persuaded Count Daru to transfer him from his comfortable post in Paris to active service in the commissariat, followed Napoleon and his army on the disastrous expedition to Russia, and in the retreat from Moscow proved himself cool, enterprising and courageous. In 1814 the Emperor abdicated, and Stendhal's official career came to an end. He claims to have refused the important posts that were offered to him and exiled himself rather than serve the Bourbons; but the facts are not quite like that; he took the oath of allegiance to the King and made attempts to get back into the public service. They failed and he returned to Milan. He still had enough money to live in a pleasant apartment and go to the opera as often as he liked; but he had neither the rank, the prestige nor the cash he had had before. Gina was cold. She told him that her husband had grown jealous on hearing of his return and that her other admirers were suspicious. She begged him for the sake of her reputation to leave Milan. He could not conceal from himself that she was finished with him, but her behavior only inflamed his passion

and at length it occurred to him that there was but one
way to regain her love. He raised three thousand francs
and turned them over to her. They went to Venice accompanied by Gina's mother, her son and a middle-aged
banker. To save appearances she insisted that Stendhal
should live in a different hotel and much to his annoyance the banker joined them when he and Gina dined
together. He couldn't think that he had any right to be
there. Here is an extract, in English, from his diary: "She
pretends that she makes me a great sacrifice in going to
Venice. I was very foolish of giving her the three thousand francs which were to pay for this tour." And ten
days later: "I have had her . . . but she talked of our
financial arrangements. There was no illusion possible
yesterday morning. Politics kills all voluptuousness in
me, apparently by drawing all the nervous fluid to the
brain."

On June 16, 1815, Napoleon was defeated at Waterloo.

In the autumn the party went back to Milan. Gina
made Stendhal take rooms in an obscure suburb. When
she gave him an assignation he went disguised in the
dead of night, throwing spies off the scent by changing carriages several times and then was admitted to
the apartment by a chambermaid. But the chambermaid,
having quarreled with her mistress or won over by the
money of Beyle, made on a sudden the startling revela-
tion that Madame's husband was not jealous at all; she
demanded all this mystery to prevent M. Beyle from en-
countering a rival, or more properly speaking, one of
his rivals, for there were many, and the maid offered to
prove it to him. Next day she hid him in a small closet
next to Gina's boudoir, and there "he saw with his own
eyes, through a keyhole, the treachery that was being
done to him, only three feet from his hiding place."
"You may think perhaps," said Beyle, "that I rushed
out of that closet in order to poniard the two of them?
Nothing of the sort. . . . I left my dark closet as quietly
as I came in, thinking only of the ridiculous side of the
adventure, laughing to myself, and also full of scorn for
the lady, and quite happy, after all, to have regained my
liberty." *

In 1821 on account of his relations with certain Italian

_____

* Quoted by Matthew Josephson from Mérimée's *Notes et Souvenirs*.

patriots Stendhal was invited by the Austrian police to leave Milan. He settled down in Paris and for most of the next nine years lived there. He had one or two dull love affairs. He frequented the salons where good talk was appreciated. He was no longer tongue-tied, but was become a witty, caustic talker, at his best with eight or ten persons, but like many good talkers inclined to monopolize the conversation. He liked to lay down the law, and took no pains to conceal his contempt for anyone who did not agree with him. In his desire to shock he indulged somewhat freely in the bawdy and the profane, and carping critics thought that to entertain or to provoke he too often forced his humor. Then came the revolution of 1830. Charles X went into exile and Louis Philippe ascended the throne. Stendhal had by this time spent the little his father had left him, and his literary efforts, for he had reverted to his old ambition to become a famous writer, brought him neither money nor reputation. His *Essay on Love* was issued in 1822, and in eleven years only seventeen copies were sold. He had tried in vain to get some kind of government post, and at last, with the change of régime, he was appointed to the consulate at Trieste; but owing to his liberal sympathies the Austrian authorities refused to accept him, and he was transferred to Civita Vecchia in the Papal States.

He took his duties lightly, and whenever possible went on a jaunt. He was an indefatigable sightseer. He found friends in Rome who made much of him. He was bored at Civita Vecchia and lonely, and at the age of fifty-one made an offer of marriage to a young girl, the daughter of his laundress and of a minor employee at the Consulate. To his mortification the offer was refused. In 1836 he persuaded his minister to give him some small job that allowed him to live in Paris for three years while someone else temporarily occupied his post. He was by then a very fat man with a very red face and long, fiercely dyed whiskers, and to cover his baldness he wore a great purple-brown wig. He dressed in the height of fashion, like a young man, and a slighting remark on the cut of his coat or the style of his pants deeply affronted him. He continued to make love, but with little success; he continued to go to parties and talk. At length he was obliged to return to Civita Vecchia and there, two years later, he had a stroke. On his recovery he asked for leave of absence to consult a famous doctor at Geneva. He went from there to Paris and resumed his old life. One day in March, 1842, he attended a large official dinner at the Ministry of Foreign Affairs and that evening, while walking along the boulevard, had another stroke. He was carried to his lodging and died next day.

The first thing that must occur to one on considering the bald facts that I have related is that, owing to the vicissitudes of his life, Stendhal acquired a variety of experience which few novelists can boast of. He was thrown into contact in a period of great change with men of all kinds and all classes, and so gained as wide a knowledge of human nature as his own idiosyncrasy permitted. For even the most observant and acute student of his fellow-creatures can only know them through the medium of his own personality. Stendhal had many limitations. He had virtues: he was sensitive, emotional, diffident, honest, talented, a hard worker when there was work to be done, brave and of a remarkable originality. He was a good friend. But his defects of character were great. His prejudices were absurd, his aims unworthy. He was distrustful (and so an easy dupe), intolerant, uncharitable, none too conscientious, fatuously vain, vain-glorious, sensual without delicacy and licentious without passion. But if we know he had these defects it is because he has told us so himself. Stendhal was not a professional author, he was hardly even a man of letters, but he wrote incessantly, and he wrote almost entirely about himself. For years he kept a journal of which great sections have come down to us, and it is evident that he wrote with no view of publication. In his early fifties he wrote an autobiography (in 500 pages) up to the age of seventeen, and this, though left unrevised at his death, he meant to be read. In it he sometimes makes himself out more important than he really was and claims to have done things he did not do, but on the whole he is truthful. He does not spare himself, and I imagine that few can read these books, and they are not easy to read since they are in parts dull and often repetitive, without asking themselves whether they would make a much better showing if they were unwise enough to expose themselves with so much frankness.

When he died only two Paris papers troubled to report the fact. It looked as though he would be entirely forgotten, and indeed he might very well have been but for the efforts of two old friends who succeeded in getting an important firm of publishers to issue an edition of his principal works. The public, however, notwithstanding two articles which the powerful critic Ste. Beuve devoted to them, remained indifferent, and it was not till a later generation that Stendhal's books began to be widely read. He had himself never doubted their survival, but he was prepared to wait till 1880 or even till 1900 to receive the appreciation that was his due. Many an author has consoled himself for the neglect of his contemporaries by a confidence that posterity will recognize his merits. It seldom does. Posterity is busy and careless, and when it concerns itself with the literary productions of the past makes it choice among those that were successful in their own day. It is only by a remote chance that a dead author is rescued from the obscurity in which he languished during his lifetime. In the case of Stendhal a professor, otherwise unknown, in his lectures at the École Normale enthusiastically praised his works, and there happened to be among his students some clever young men who later made a name for themselves. They read them, and finding in them something that suited the climate of opinion at the time prevalent among the young, became fanatical admirers. The ablest of these young men was Hippolyte Taine, and many years later, by which time he was become a well-known and influential man of letters, he wrote a celebrated article in which he called Stendhal the greatest psychologist of all the ages. Since then an immense amount has been written about him, and it is generally agreed now that he is one of the three greatest novelists that France produced in the nineteenth century.

His fame rests on one passage in his *Essay on Love* and on two novels. Of these *The Charterhouse of Parma* is perhaps the more agreeable to read, and it has two characters that are captivating. The description of the Battle of Waterloo is justly famous. But *The Red and the Black* is more striking, more original and more significant. It is because of this that Zola called Stendhal the father of the Naturalistic School, and that Bourget and André Gide have claimed him (incorrectly) as the originator of the psychological novel. It is truly an amazing book.

Stendhal was always more interested in himself than in anyone else, and he was always the hero of his novels. Julien of *The Red and the Black* is the kind of man Stendhal would have liked to be. He made him attractive to women and successful in winning their devoted love as he would himself have given everything to be and never was. He made him achieve his ends with them by just those methods that he had thought out for himself and that consistently failed. He made him a brilliant talker, though very wisely never gave an example of his brilliance, but only affirmed it. He gave him his own good memory, his own courage, his own timidity, his own inferiority complex, his own amibition, sensitiveness, calculating brains, his own suspiciousness and vanity and quickness to take offense, his own unscrupulousness and his own ingratitude. Never has an author, I think, in putting himself into a character, drawn a portrait of someone so vile, so base, so worthless, so hateful.

It is curious that with the exception of his description of Waterloo, at which he was not present, Stendhal seems to have made little use in his fiction of his experiences when in the service of Napoleon. One would have supposed that the great events of which he was at least a witness would have suggested to him a theme that he would have felt called upon to deal with. The reader will remember that when he wanted to write plays he looked for subjects in the plays he was seeing: Stendhal seems to have had no gift for making up a story out of his own head, and he took the plot of *The Red and the Black* from newspaper reports of a trial that at the time excited interest. In the introductions to these novels I have taken care not to divulge the plot, but in this case I cannot help giving at least an inkling of it if I want to discuss the book at all. This is the incident that Stendhal made use of: a young seminarist called Antoine Berthet was tutor in the house of a M. Michoud, then in that of a M. de Cordon. He tried to seduce or did seduce the wife of the first and the daughter of the second. He was discharged. He tried then to resume his studies for the priesthood, but owing to his bad reputation no seminary would receive him. He took it into his head that the Michouds were responsible for this, and in revenge shot Madame Michoud while she was in church, and then himself. The wound was not fatal and he was tried; he attempted to save himself at the expense of the unfortunate woman, but was condemned to death.

This ugly, sordid story appealed to Stendhal; he looked upon Berthet's act as a fine crime (*un beau crime*) and as the reaction of a strong, rebellious nature against the social order. He attempted to give it elevation by putting the sufferers from Julien's malice in a higher station, and by ascribing to his hero more intelligence, more force of character and more courage than were possessed by the wretched Berthet. But it remains a sordid story and Julien base. He is, however, very much alive and the novel is passionately interesting. Julien, a working-class boy devoured with envy and hatred of those born in a more privileged class, is representative of a type that occurs in every generation. Here, when we catch our first glimpse of him, is how Stendhal describes him: "He was a small young man of eighteen or nineteen, weakly to look at, with irregular, delicate features and an aquiline nose. His large black eyes, which in moments of tranquillity, suggested reflection and fire, were lit up at that instant with an expression of the fiercest hate. His dark chestnut hair, growing very low, gave him a small forehead and in moments of anger a look of wickedness. . . . His slender, well-set figure suggested lightness rather than vigor." Not an attractive portrait, but a good one because it does not predispose the reader in Julien's favor. The principal character in a novel naturally enlists the reader's sympathy, and Stendhal, having chosen a villain for his hero, had to take care from the start that his readers should not sympathize with him overmuch. On the other hand he had to interest them in him. He could not afford to make him too repulsive, so he modifies his first description by dwelling repeatedly on his fine eyes, his graceful figure and his delicate hands. At times he describes him as positively beautiful. But he does not forget from time to time to call your attention to the malaise he excites in persons who come in contact with him, and to the suspicion with which he is regarded by all save those who have most cause to be on their guard against him.

Madame de Rênal, the mother of the children he is engaged to teach, is a beautifully drawn portrait of a character most difficult to depict. She is a good wife, a good mother, a good woman, charming, virtuous, sincere; and the narrative of her growing love for Julien, with its fears and hesitations, and the flaming passion which it becomes, is masterly. She is one of the most touching creatures of fiction. The patrician Mathilde de la Môle is unbelievable. Stendhal had never moved familiarly in good society, and he did not know how well-bred people behaved. It is a parvenu's notion that persons of noble birth are perpetually occupied with their nobility. He thought Mademoiselle de la Môle's insolence was aristocratic; it was merely vulgar. Her actions are a tissue of absurdities.

Stendhal hated the flowery manner of writing Chateaubriand had made fashionable, and which a hundred lesser writers assiduously copied. His aim was to put down whatever he had to say as plainly and accurately as he could, without frills, without rhetorical flourishes or picturesque verbiage. He said (probably not quite truly) that before starting to write he read a page of the Code of Civil Law in order to chasten his language. He eschewed description of scenery and such like ornaments as were popular in his day. The cold, lucid, self-controlled style he adopted wonderfully increases the horror of the story and adds to its enthralling interest. I don't see how the parts which deal with Julien's life with the Rênals and at the seminary could be better; it is when the scene is changed to Paris and the mansion of the Marquis de la Môle that I, for my part, find myself incredulous. I am asked to accept more improbabilities than I can swallow and to interest myself in episodes that are pointless. Stendhal succeeded in writing after a realistic fashion, but no one, however hard he tries, can fail to be influenced by the psychic atmosphere of his time. Romanticism was rampant. Stendhal, notwithstanding his appreciation of the good sense and urbane culture of the eighteenth century, was profoundly affected by it. He was fascinated by the ruthless men of the Italian Renaissance who were troubled neither by scruple nor remorse, and hesitated at no crime to satisfy their ambition, gratify their lust or avenge their honor. He prized their strength of will, their scorn for convention and their freedom of soul. It is because of this romantic predilection that the last half of *The Red and the Black* fails to convince.

It is when Julien, by dissimulation, diplomacy and

self-restraint is in sight of achieving all his ambition craved that Stendhal makes what I can only look upon as a great error. We are told that Julien is clever and immensely cunning, and yet to recommend himself to his future father-in-law he asks him to write to Madame de Rênal, the honest woman he seduced, for a certificate of character. Should it not have occurred to him that either she must hate him for the harm he has done her, in which case she might want to revenge herself, or still loves him, in which case she would be unlikely to welcome the news that he is going to marry someone else? We know her to be a conscientious woman. It might have crossed his mind that she might think it her duty to expose his lack of principle. That is what she does. She writes a letter in which she tells the plain truth about him. Instead of denying it and ascribing it to the pique of a discarded mistress, he takes pistols and drives down to where she lives and shoots her. No explanation is given. He acts on impulse, and we know that Stendhal had an inordinate admiration for the impulsive act which was a manifestation of passion; very well; but we have been shown from the beginning of the novel that the strength of Julien consisted precisely in his immense self-control. His passions, envy, hatred, pride, vanity, never dominated him, and his lust, the strongest passion of them all, was, as with Stendhal himself, not so much a matter of urgent desire as of the satisfaction of vanity. At the crisis of the book Julien does the fatal thing in a novel: he acts out of character.

Stendhal had followed the story of Antoine Berthet very closely and he had without doubt the intention of following it to the end; but he seems not to have noticed that, first, he had made Julien a very different man from the blackmailer who served as his model, and second, that Berthet was persuaded that Madame Michoud had ruined his chances of making a career. He had a grievance; Julien had none. If Madame de Rênal blasted his ambitious hopes he had only his own stupidity to blame, and he was very far from being stupid; and he held besides in his hand trump cards that would have enabled him to counteract the effects of his unaccountable mistake. The fact is that Stendhal had little power of invention, and so failed in devising a means of ending his book in a manner that the reader can accept as probable. But as I have pointed out, no novel is perfect, owing partly to the natural inadequacy of the form and partly to the deficiencies of the human being who writes it. Notwithstanding, *The Red and the Black* remains one of the most remarkable ever written. To read it is a unique experience.

EMILY BRONTË

and

WUTHERING HEIGHTS

PATRICK PRUNTY was born in County Down in 1777. His father, a farmer, had ten children to feed on the produce of the few acres of land he owned, and Patrick went to work as soon as he was old enough, first as a weaver and then as a teacher in a village school, and after that as tutor in a clergyman's family. He was ambitious and eager to get on in the world; and with the help of the clergyman, his employer, he managed to raise enough money to go to Cambridge. He was then twenty-five, old to enter a university, a tall, very strong young man, handsome and vain of his good looks. When at St. John's College he changed his plebeian name of Prunty into Brontë, the name of a town in Sicily which with an exclusive estate had been recently granted to Nelson as a duchy by Ferdinand IV. Patrick Brontë took his degree, was ordained, and after occupying various curacies settled down for five years in one at Hartshead. There he married Maria Branwell, the daughter of a Cornish trader. He had two children by her, Maria and Elizabeth. Then he moved to another curacy near Bradford, where Mrs. Brontë had four more children. They were named Charlotte, Patrick Branwell, Emily and Anne. In 1820 the Rev. Patrick Brontë was appointed to the living, a poor living worth £200 a year, of Haworth, a Yorkshire village, and here he remained, his ambition, one must suppose, satisfied, till his death. He never went back to Ireland to see the parents, the brothers and sisters he had left there.

In 1821 his wife died, and about a year later, after two or three unsuccessful attempts to marry again, he induced her elder sister, Elizabeth Branwell, to leave Penzance, where she lived, to come to look after his children.

Haworth Parsonage was a small stone house near the church on the brow of the steep hill down which the village straggled. The floors and the stairs were of stone, cold and damp, and Miss Branwell for fear of catching cold always went about the house in pattens. There was a parlor, a study for Mr. Brontë, a kitchen and a storeroom on the first floor and four bedrooms and a lobby on the second. There were no carpets except in the parlor and the study and no curtains to the windows because Mr. Brontë dreaded fire. In Mr. Brontë's study there were mahogany tables and chairs covered with horsehair, but the other rooms were sparsely furnished. Back and front of the house was a strip of garden and on the two sides the graveyard. All about, stretching as far as eyes could reach, were the bleak moors.

Over these moors Mr. Brontë walked long and far. He was a man who shunned company and with the exception of a neighboring parson who sometimes came down the hills to pay a visit, saw no one except his churchwardens and his parishioners. Even before his wife's death he had taken to having his meals in his study by himself, and this habit he retained for the rest of his life. At eight o'clock at night he read family prayers, and at nine locked and barred the front door. As he passed the room in which his children were sitting he told them not to be late, and halfway up the stairs stopped to wind the clock. He was of a violent temper, selfish, "stern and peremptory." Having married his wife, he treated her with coldness and neglect; he did not like his children and was irritable when they interrupted him; they were delicate, but he wished to make them hardy and indifferent to the pleasures of eating and dress; he would not eat meat himself and did not allow them to eat it, and they were fed, as he had been in his childhood, chiefly on potatoes. He, the son of a poverty-stricken Irish farmer, would not let them associate with the village children, and they were driven to sit in the "children's study," the cold little lobby on the second floor, reading or whispering low in order not to disturb their father who, when annoyed or displeased, maintained a sullen silence. He taught them their lessons in the morning, and Miss Branwell, after she joined them, taught them sewing and housework.

They amused themselves by wandering about the moor and by writing plays, poems, essays and romances. In

1824 Maria and Elizabeth and then Charlotte and Emily were sent to a school at Cowan Bridge which had recently been established to give an education to the daughters of poor clergymen. The place was unhealthy, the food bad and the administration incompetent. The two elder girls died, and Charlotte and Emily, whose health was affected, were, though not immediately, removed. Such schooling as they got after that they owed to their aunt. They read a great deal, and their reading, limited to the English classics, was solid—Shakespeare and Milton, of course, Pope, whom Charlotte at all events didn't admire, Scott, Byron and Wordsworth; Boswell, Johnson's *Lives of the Poets* and *Moore's Life of Byron*. The only fiction they read was Scott, for "all novels after his," said Charlotte, "are worthless."

Branwell was looked upon as the clever one of the family, and his father thought more of him than of his three girls. He would not send him to school, but undertook to educate him himself. The boy had a precocious talent, and his manners were engaging. His friend, F. H. Grundy, thus describes him: "He was insignificantly small —one of his life's trials. He had a mass of red hair, which he wore brushed high off his forehead—to help his height, I fancy—a great, bumpy, intellectual forehead, nearly half the size of the whole facial contour; small ferrety eyes, deep sunk and still farther hidden by the never removed spectacles, prominent nose, but weak lower features. He had a downcast look, which never varied, save for a rapid momentary glance at long intervals. Small and thin of person, he was the reverse of attractive at first sight." He had parts, and his sisters admired him and expected him to do great things. He was a brilliant, eager talker, and from some Irish ancestor, for his father was a morose, silent man, he had inherited a gift for social intercourse and an agreeable loquacity. When a traveler putting up for the night at the *Black Bull* seemed lonely, the landlord would ask him: "Do you want someone to help you with your bottle, Sir? If so, I'll send up for Patrick." Branwell was always glad to be of service.

When Charlotte was sixteen she went to school once more, this time at Roe Head, and was happy there, but after a year she came home again to teach her two younger sisters. The family was very poor, and the girls had nothing to look forward to, for Miss Branwell was leaving the little money she had to her amusing nephew, and so they had decided that the only way they could earn a living was by training themselves to be governesses or school teachers. Branwell reached the age of eighteen, and a decision had to be made on what trade or profession he was to adopt. He had some facility for drawing, as his sisters had too, and he was eager to become a painter. It was settled that he should go to London and study at the Royal Academy. It appears to be uncertain whether he went or not, but the *Encyclopædia Britannica* says he did and there "indulged in a glorious month of extravagance," after which he came home again. "His art studies were continued for a time at Leeds, but it may be assumed that no commissions came to him, and at last he became tutor to the son of a Mr. Postlethwaite at Barrow-in-Furness. Ten months later he was a booking clerk at Sowerby Bridge Station on the Leeds and Manchester Railway and later at Luddenden Foot." He was discharged for gross neglect of his duties.

Meanwhile Charlotte had returned to the school at Roe Head as a teacher and had taken Emily with her as a pupil. But Emily became so desperately homesick that she fell ill and had to be sent home. Anne, who was of a calmer, more submissive temper, took her place. But Charlotte's health failed after three years—notwithstanding Mr. Brontë's efforts to make his children hardy they remained delicate—and she went back to Haworth.

She was then twenty-two. Branwell was not only a source of worry, but a source of expense; and Charlotte, as soon as she was well enough, felt herself obliged to take a situation as a nursery governess. It was not work she liked. The fact is that neither she nor her sisters liked children any more than their father did. "I find it so hard to repel the rude familiarity of children," she wrote to an intimate friend. She hated to be in a dependent position, and was continually on the lookout for affronts. So far as one can judge from her letters she seems to have expected to be asked to do as a favor what her employers quite naturally supposed they could demand as a right. She left after three months and went back to the parsonage, but about two years later took another situation; she was moderately happy but, as she wrote to the same friend: "No one but myself can tell how hard a governess's life is to me—for no one but myself is aware how utterly averse my whole mind and nature are for the employment." She had long been toying with the idea of keeping a school of her own, with her two sisters, and now she took it up again; her employers, who seem to have been very kind, decent people, encouraged her, but suggested that before she could hope to be successful she must acquire certain qualifications. Though she could read French she could not speak it, and knew no German, so she decided that she must go abroad to learn languages. Her aunt advanced money and, accompanied by her sister Emily, she went to Brussels where she became a pupil of the Pensionnat Héger. The two girls were recalled to England after ten months by the illness of Miss Branwell. She died, and having disinherited Branwell owing to his bad behavior, left the little she had to her three nieces. It was enough for them to carry out the plan they had so long discussed of having a school of their own, but since their father was old and his sight failing they made up their minds to set it up at the parsonage. Charlotte did not think she was sufficiently equipped and so accepted Monsieur Héger's offer to go back to Brussels to teach English. Anne was in a situation as a governess and Emily stayed at home. Charlotte spent a year in Brussels and on returning to Haworth the three sisters issued prospectuses, and Charlotte wrote to her friends asking them to recommend the school they intended to start. No pupils came.

They had been writing off and on since they were children, and in 1846 the three of them issued a volume of verse at their own expense under the names of Currer, Ellis and Acton Bell. It cost them £50, and two copies were sold. Each of them then wrote a novel: Charlotte's (Currer Bell) was called *The Professor,* Emily's (Ellis Bell) *Wuthering Heights* and Anne's (Acton Bell) *Agnes Grey*. They were refused by publisher after publisher, but when Smith, Elder & Co., to whom Charlotte's *The Professor* had finally been sent, returned it they wrote to say that they would be glad to consider a longer novel by her. She was finishing one, and within a month was able to send it to the publishers. They accepted it. It was called *Jane Eyre*. Emily's novel and Anne's had also at last been accepted by a publisher, Newby by name, "on terms somewhat impoverishing to the two authors," and they had corrected the proofs before Charlotte sent *Jane*

Eyre to Smith, Elder & Co. Though the reviews of *Jane Eyre* were not particularly good, readers liked it and it turned out to be a bestseller. Mr. Newby upon this tried to persuade the public that *Wuthering Heights* and *Agnes Grey,* which he then published together in three volumes, were by the author of *Jane Eyre.* They made, however, no impression, and indeed were regarded by a number of critics as early and immature work by Currer Bell.

This was in 1848. Now to go back a little: in 1842 Branwell was engaged as a tutor by a Mr. Edmund Robinson, a wealthy clergyman, in whose family Anne was at the time employed as a governess. Mr. Robinson was an elderly invalid with a youngish wife and Branwell, though she was seventeen years older than he, fell in love with her and she with him. Their relations are so delicately alluded to that it is impossible to tell whether or not he became her lover. Anyhow, whatever they were, they were discovered. Branwell was sent packing and Mr. Robinson ordered him "never to see again the mother of his children, never set foot in her home, never write or speak to her." Branwell "stormed, raved, swore he could not live without her; cried out against her for staying with her husband. Then prayed the sick man might die soon; they would yet be happy." Branwell had always drunk too much; now in his distress he took to eating opium. It appears, however, that he was able to communicate with Mrs. Robinson, and some months after his dismissal they met at Harrogate. "It is said that she proposed a flight together, ready to forfeit all her grandeur. It was Branwell who advised patience and a little longer waiting." Suddenly he received a letter to announce the death of Mr. Robinson; "he fair danced down the churchyard as if he were out of his mind; he was so fond of that woman," someone told Emily's biographer.

"The next morning he rose, dressed himself with care and prepared for a journey, but before he had even set out from Haworth two men came riding to the village posthaste. They sent for Branwell and when he arrived, in a great state of excitement, one of the riders dismounted and went with him into the Black Bull." He brought a message from the widow begging him not to come near her again, for if she even saw him once she would lose her fortune and the custody of her children. Branwell proceeded to drink himself to death. When he knew the end was come, wanting to die standing, he insisted upon getting up. He had only been in bed a day. Charlotte was so upset that she had to be led away, but her father, Anne and Emily looked on while he rose to his feet and after a struggle that lasted twenty minutes died, as he wished, standing. I should warn the reader that this account of Branwell's love and death is such as was gathered from persons who may be supposed to have known the facts; but the author of the article on the Brontës in the English *Dictionary of National Biography,* writing many years after the event, claims that there is no truth in it. Perhaps with a little more imagination and less bias against Branwell he might not have been so positive.

Anyhow Branwell died, and Emily never went out of doors after the Sunday following his death. She was ill. "Her reserved nature occasions me great uneasiness," Charlotte wrote to a friend. "It is useless to question her; you get no answers. It is still more useless to recommend remedies; they are never adopted." When a doctor was sent for she would not see him. She made no complaints; she wanted neither sympathy nor help. She would let no one do anything for her, and when anyone tried resented it. One morning she got up, dressed herself and began to sew; she was short of breath and her eyes were glazed, but she went on working. She grew steadily worse and at midday asked for a doctor. It was too late. At two she died. Anne died a few months later.

Charlotte had been at work on another novel, *Shirley,* between the death of Branwell and that of Emily, but she put it aside to nurse Anne and did not finish it till after her death. She went to London in 1849 and in 1850 and was made much of; she was introduced to Thackeray and had her portrait painted by George Richmond. During 1852 she wrote *Villette,* and in 1854 she married. She had had several offers of marriage before, mostly from her father's curates, for his failing health had obliged him to have help in his parish; but Emily discouraged suitors (her sisters called her the Major because of the effective way she dealt with them), and her father disapproved, so she refused them all. It was however a curate of her father's whom she at last married. He had been attached to her for several years and, with Emily gone and her father resigned, she at last accepted him. They were married in June and in the following March she died of what is primly described as an "illness incidental to childbirth."

So the Rev. Patrick Brontë, having buried his wife, her sister and his six children, was left to eat his meals alone in the solitude he liked, walk on the moors as far as his waning strength permitted, read his books, preach his sermons and wind up the clock on his way to bed. There is a photograph of him in his old age. A man in a black suit with an immense white choker round his neck, with white hair cut short, a fine brow and a large straight nose, a tight mouth and ill-tempered eyes behind his spectacles. He died at Haworth at the age of eighty-four.

It is not without intention that in writing of Emily Brontë's *Wuthering Heights* I have said so much about her father, her brother and her sister Charlotte, for in the books written about the family it is of them that we hear most. Emily and Anne hardly come into the picture; Anne was a gentle, pretty little thing, but insignificant, and her talent was small. Emily was very different. She is a strange, mysterious and shadowy figure. She is never seen directly, but reflected, as it were, in a moorland pool. You have to guess what sort of woman she was from an allusion here and there and from scattered anecdotes. She was aloof, a harsh, uncomfortable creature, and when you hear of her giving over to unrestrained gaiety, as she sometimes did on walks over the moors, it makes you uneasy. Charlotte had friends, Anne had friends, Emily had none.

Mary Robinson describes her at fifteen as "a tall, long-armed girl, full grown, elastic as to tread; with a slight figure that looked queenly in her best dresses, but loose and boyish when she slouched over the moors, whistling to the dogs, and taking long strides over the rough earth. A tall, thin, loose-jointed girl—not ugly, but with irregular features and a pallid thick complexion. Her dark hair was naturally beautiful, and in later days looked well, loosely fastened with a tall comb at the back of her head; but in 1833 she wore it in an unbecoming tight curl and frizz. She had beautiful eyes of a hazel colour." Like her father, her brother and her sisters she wore spectacles. She had an aquiline nose and a large, expressive, prominent mouth. She dressed regardless of fashion, with leg-of-mutton sleeves long after they had ceased to be worn;

in straight long skirts clinging to her lanky figure. She was miserable away from home. She hated Brussels. Friends tried to be nice to the two girls and asked them to spend Sundays and holidays at their house, but they were so shy that to go was agony for them, and after a while their hosts thought it kinder not to invite them. It was natural that they should be shy; they had been brought up in seclusion and had had little experience of social life; but shyness is a somewhat complicated state of mind, there is diffidence in it, but also conceit, and from this Emily at least was not free.

At school during the hours of recreation the two sisters always walked together and generally in silence. When they were spoken to Charlotte answered. Emily rarely spoke to anyone. Monsieur Héger thought her intelligent, but so stubborn that she would listen to no reason when it interfered with her wishes or beliefs. He found her egotistical, exacting, and with Charlotte tyrannical. But he recognized that there was something unusual in her. She should have been a man, he said, "Her strong imperious will would never have been daunted by opposition or difficulty; never have given way but with life."

When Emily went back to Haworth after her aunt's death it was for good. She never left it again.

She got up in the morning before anybody else and did the roughest part of the day's work before Tabby, the maid, who was old and frail, came down. She did the household ironing and most of the cooking. She made the bread, and the bread was good. While she kneaded the dough she would glance at the book propped up before her. "Those who worked with her in the kitchen, young girls called in to help in stress of business, remember how she would keep a scrap of paper, a pencil at her side, and how when the moment came that she could pause in her cooking or her ironing, she would jot down some impatient thought and then resume her work. With these girls she was always friendly and hearty—'pleasant, sometimes quite jovial like a boy! So genial and kind, a little masculine,' say my informants, 'but of strangers she was exceedingly timid, and if the butcher's boy or the baker's man came to the kitchen door she would be off like a bird into the hall or the parlor till she heard their hobnails clumping down the path.' " I think that much in her behavior that was strange to her contemporaries would be clear to a psychiatrist today.

Someone told Mrs. Gaskell, Charlotte Brontë's biographer, that Emily "never showed regard to any human creature; all her love was reserved for animals." She liked them wild and intractable. Someone gave her a bulldog called Keeper, and concerning him Mrs. Gaskell tells a curious anecdote. I will give it in her own words: "Keeper was faithful to the depths of his nature so long as he was with friends; but he who struck him with a stick or whip, roused the relentless nature of the brute, who flew at his throat forthwith, and held him there till one or the other was at the point of death. Now Keeper's household fault was this. He loved to steal upstairs, and stretch his square, tawny limbs on the comfortable beds, covered over with delicate white counterpanes. But the cleanliness of the parsonage arrangements was perfect; and this habit of Keeper's was so objectionable, that Emily, in reply to Tabby's remonstrances, declared that, if he was found again transgressing, she herself, in defiance of warning and his well-known ferocity of nature, would beat him so severely that he would never offend again. In the gathering dusk of an autumn evening, Tabby came, half-triumphantly, half-tremblingly, but in great wrath, to tell Emily that Keeper was lying on the best bed, in drowsy voluptuousness. Charlotte saw Emily's whitening face and set mouth, but dared not speak to interfere; no one dared when Emily's eyes glowed in that manner out of the paleness of her face, and when her lips were compressed into stone. She went upstairs, and Tabby and Charlotte stood in the gloomy passage below, full of the dark shadows of coming night. Downstairs came Emily, dragging after her the unwilling Keeper, his hind legs set in a heavy attitude of resistance, held by the 'scuff of his neck,' but growling low and savagely all the time. The watchers would fain have spoken, but durst not, for fear of taking off Emily's attention, and causing her to avert her head for a moment from the enraged brute. She let him go, planted in a dark corner at the bottom of the stairs; no time was there to fetch stick or rod, for fear of the strangling clutch at her throat—her bare clenched fist struck against his red fierce eyes, before he had time to make his spring, and in the language of the turf, she 'punished' him till his eyes were swelled up, and the half-blind, stupefied beast was led to his accustomed lair, to have his swollen head fomented and cared for by the very Emily herself."

Charlotte wrote of her: "Disinterested and energetic she certainly is; and if she be not quite so tractable and open to conviction as I could wish, I must remember perfection is not the lot of humanity."

It is evident that Charlotte did not quite know what to make of *Wuthering Heights;* she had no notion that her sister had produced a book of astonishing originality and one compared with which her own were commonplace. She felt compelled to apologize for it. When it was proposed to republish it she undertook to edit it. "I am likewise compelling myself to read it over, for the first time of opening the book since my sister's death. Its power fills me with renewed admiration; but yet I am oppressed: the reader is scarcely ever permitted a taste of unalloyed pleasure; every beam of sunshine is poured down through black bars of threatening cloud; every page is surcharged with a sort of moral electricity; and the writer was unconscious of all this—nothing could make her conscious of it." And again: "If the auditor of her work, when read in manuscript, shuddered under the grinding influence of natures so relentless and implacable —of spirits so lost and fallen; if it was complained that the mere hearing of certain vivid and fearful scenes banished sleep by night, and disturbed mental peace by day, Ellis Bell would wonder what was meant, and suspect the complainant of affectation. Had she but lived, her mind would of itself have grown like a strong tree— loftier, straighter, wider-spreading—and its matured fruits would have attained a mellower ripeness and sunnier bloom; but on that mind time and experience alone could work; to the influence of other intellects it was not amenable."

One is inclined to think that Charlotte little knew her sister. *Wuthering Heights* is an extraordinary book. It is a very bad one. It is a very fine one. It is ugly. It has beauty. It is a terrible, an agonizing, a passionate book. Some have thought it impossible that a clergyman's daughter who led a retired, humdrum life and knew few people and nothing of the world could have written it. This seems to me absurd. *Wuthering Heights* is wildly romantic: now romanticism eschews the patient observation of realism; it revels in the unbridled flight of the imagination and indulges, sometimes with gusto, sometimes with gloom, in horror, mystery, fearful passions and deeds of violence. It is an escape from reality. Given Emily Brontë's character, of which I have tried to give some indication, and fierce, repressed passions, which what we know of her suggests, *Wuthering Heights* is just the sort of book one would have expected her to write. But on the face of it, it is much more the sort of book that her scapegrace brother Branwell might have written, and a number of people have been able to persuade themselves that he had either in whole or in part in fact done so. One of them, Francis Grundy, wrote: "Patrick Brontë declared to me, and what his sister said bore out the assertion, that he wrote a great part of *Wuthering Heights* himself. . . . The weird fancies of diseased genius with which he used to entertain me in our long talks at Luddendenfoot, reappear in the pages of the novel, and I am inclined to believe that the very plot was his invention rather than his sister's." On one occasion two of Branwell's friends, Dearden and Leyland by name, arranged to meet him at an inn on the road to Keighley to read their poetical effusions to one another, and this is what Dearden some twenty years later wrote to the Halifax *Guardian*: "I read the first act of *The Demon Queen;* but when Branwell dived into his hat—the usual receptacle of his fugitive scraps—where he supposed he had deposited his manuscript poem, he found he had by mistake placed there a number of stray leaves of a novel on which he had been trying his 'prentice hand.' Chagrined at the disappointment he had caused, he was about to return the papers to his hat, when both friends earnestly pressed him to read them, as they felt a curiosity to see how he could wield the pen of a novelist. After some hesitation, he complied with the request, and riveted our attention for about an hour, dropping each sheet, when read, into his hat. The story broke off abruptly in the middle of a sentence, and he gave us the sequel, *viva voce,* together with the real names of the prototypes of his characters; but, as some of these persons are still living, I refrain from pointing them out to the public. He said he had not yet fixed upon a title for his production, and was afraid he would never be able to meet with a publisher who would have the hardihood to usher it into the world. The scene of the fragment which Branwell read, and the characters introduced in it—so far as they developed—were the same as those in *Wuthering Heights*, which Charlotte Brontë confidently asserts was the production of her sister Emily."

Now this is either a pack of lies or it is true. Charlotte despised and within the bounds of Christian charity hated her brother; but as we know, Christian charity has always been able to make allowances for a lot of good honest hatred, and Charlotte's unsupported word cannot be accepted. She may, as people often do, have persuaded herself to believe what she wanted to believe. The story is circumstantial, and it is odd that anyone for no particular reason should have invented it. What is the explanation? There is none. It has been suggested that Branwell wrote the first four chapters, and then, drunk and doped as he was, gave it up, whereupon Emily took it over. The argument adduced is that these chapters are written in a more stilted style than the rest of the novel. That I cannot see. The whole book is very badly written in the pseudo-literary manner that the amateur is apt to affect. When the amateur, and it must be remembered that Emily Brontë had never written a book before, sits down to write he thinks he must use grand words rather than ordinary ones. It is only by practice that he learns to write simply. The main part of the story is told by a Yorkshire servant and she expresses herself in a way that no human being could. Emily Brontë was perhaps aware that she was putting words into Mrs. Dean's mouth that she could hardly have known, and to explain it makes her say that she has in the course of her service had the opportunity to read a number of books, but even at that the pretentiousness of her discourse is appalling. She never *tries* to do a thing, but *endeavors* or *essays,* she never *leaves* a room but *quits* it, she never *meets* anybody but *encounters* him. I should have said that whoever wrote the first chapters wrote the rest, and if in the early ones there is somewhat more pomposity in the writing I surmise that this is owning to a not unsuccessful attempt on Emily's part to show that Lockwood was a silly, conceited man.

I have read somewhere the conjecture that if it was Branwell who wrote the beginning of the novel his intention was to make Lockwood take a much greater part in the action. There is indeed a hint that he was attracted by the younger Catherine, and it is obvious that if he had fallen in love with her a complication would have been added to the intrigue. As it is, Lockwood is merely a nuisance. The novel is very clumsily constructed. But is this surprising? Emily Brontë had never written one before and she had a complicated story to tell dealing with two generations. This is always a difficult thing to do because the author has to give some sort of unity to a narrative that concerns two sets of characters and two sets of events; and he must be careful not to allow the interest of one set to overshadow the interest of the other. He has also to compress the passage of years into a period of time that can be accepted by the reader with a comprehensive glance as one seizes in a single view the whole of a vast fresco. I do not suppose that Emily Brontë deliberately thought out how to get a unity of impression into a straggling story, but I think she must have wondered how to make it coherent, and it may have occurred to her that she could best do this by making one character narrate the long succession of events to another. It is a convenient way of telling a story, and she did not invent it. Its disadvantage is, as I pointed out just now, that it is almost impossible to maintain a conversational manner when the narrator has to *tell* a number of things, descriptions of scenery for instance, which no sane person would think of doing. And of course if you have a narrator (Mrs. Dean) you must have a listener (Lockwood). It is possible that an experienced novelist might have found a better way of telling the story of *Wuthering Heights,* but I cannot persuade myself that if Emily Brontë used it it was because she was working on a foundation of someone else's invention.

But more than that, I think that Emily Brontë's method might have been expected of her when you consider her extreme, her morbid shyness and reticence. What were the alternatives? One was to write the novel from the standpoint of omniscience, as for instance *Middlemarch* and *Madame Bovary* were written. I think it would have shocked her harsh, uncompromising virtue to tell the outrageous story as a creation of her own; and if she had, moreover, she could hardly have avoided giving some account of Heathcliff during the years he spent away from Wuthering Heights, years during which he managed to acquire an education and make money. She couldn't do this because she simply didn't know how he had done it. The fact the reader is asked to accept is hard to believe, and she was content to state it and leave it at that. Another alternative was to have the story narrated to her, Emily Brontë, by Mrs. Dean, say, and tell it then in the first person; but I suspect that that too would have brought her into a contact with the reader too close for her quivering sensibility. By having the story in its beginning told by Lockwood and unfolded to Lockwood by Mrs. Dean she hid herself behind, as it were, a double mask. The Rev. Patrick Brontë told Mrs. Gaskell a story which in this connection has some significance. When his children were young, desiring to find out something of their natures which their timidity concealed from him, he made each one in turn put on an old mask, under the cover of which they could answer more freely the questions he put to them. When he asked Charlotte what was the best book in the world she answered: The Bible; but when he asked Emily what he had best do with her troublesome brother Branwell, she said: "Reason with him; and when he won't listen to reason, whip him."

And why did Emily need to hide herself when she wrote this powerful, terrible book? I think because she disclosed in it her innermost instincts. She looked deep into the well of loneliness of her heart and saw there undisclosable secrets of which, notwithstanding, her impulse as a writer drove her to unburden herself. It is said that her imagination was kindled by the weird stories her father used to tell of the Ireland of his youth and by the tales of Hoffman which she learned to read when she went to school in Belgium and which she continued to read, we are told, back at the parsonage seated on a hearthrug by the fire with her arm around Keeper's neck. Charlotte was at pains to state that Emily, whatever she had heard of them, had no communication with the people round her who might be supposed to have suggested the characters of her novel. I am willing to believe that this is true, and I am willing to believe that she found in the stories of mystery and horror of the German romantic writers something that appealed to her own fierce nature; but I think she found Heathcliff and Catherine

Earnshaw in the hidden depths of her own soul. It may be that in the lesser characters—Linton and his sister, Earnshaw's wife and Heathcliff's—objects of her disdain for their weakness and frailty, she found hints in persons she had known, but readers seldom give an author credit for a power of invention and it is just as likely that she created them out of her own overbearing and contemptuous imagination. I think she was herself Catherine Earnshaw, wild, tempestuous, passionate; and I think she was Heathcliff.

Is it strange that she should have put herself into the two chief characters of her book? Not at all. We are none of us all of a piece; more than one person dwells within us, often in uneasy companionship with his fellows; and the peculiarity of the writer of fiction is that he has the power to objectify the diverse persons of which he is compounded into individual characters: his misfortune is that he cannot bring to life characters, however necessary to his story they may be, in which there is no part of himself. It is not only not uncommon for an author writing his first novel, as *Wuthering Heights* was, to make himself his principal character, it is not uncommon either that in his theme there will be something of wish-fulfilment. It becomes then a confession of the reveries, on solitary walks or in wakeful hours at night, in which he has imagined himself saint or sinner, great lover or great statesman, heroic general or cold-blooded murderer; and it is because there is a lot of absurdity in most people's reveries that there is a great deal of nonsense in most writers' first novels. I think *Wuthering Heights* is just such a confession.

I think Emily Brontë put the whole of herself into Heathcliff. She gave him, I think, her violent rage, her sexuality, vehement but frustrated, her passion of unsatisfied love, her jealousy, her hatred and contempt of human beings, her cruelty, her sadism. The reader will remember the incident when with so little reason with her naked fist she beat the face of the dog she loved as perhaps she loved no human being. There is another curious incident related by Charlotte's friend, Ellen Nussey: "She enjoyed leading Charlotte where she would not dare go of her own free will. Charlotte had a mortal dread of unknown animals, and it was Emily's pleasure to lead her into close vicinity, and then tell her of how and what she

had done, laughing at her horror with great amusement."
I think Emily loved Catherine Earnshaw with Heathcliff's
masculine, purely animal love, and I think she laughed, as
she had laughed at Charlotte's fears, when as Heathcliff she kicked and trampled on Earnshaw and dashed
his head repeatedly against the stone flags, and I think she
laughed when, as Heathcliff, she hit the younger Catherine in the face and heaped humiliations upon her; I think
it gave her a thrill of release when she bullied, reviled
and browbeat the persons of her invention because in
real life she suffered such bitter mortification in the
company of her fellow creatures; and I think, as Catherine, doubling the rôles, as it were, though she fought
Heathcliff, though she despised him, though she knew
him for the evil thing he was, she loved him with her
body and soul, she exulted in her power over him, she
felt they were kin (as indeed they were if I am right in
supposing they were both Emily Brontë), and since
there is in the sadist often something of the masochist
too, she was fascinated by his violence, his brutality and
his untamed nature.

But I have said enough. *Wuthering Heights* is not a
book to talk about; it is a book to read. It is easy to
find fault with it; it is very imperfect; and yet it has what
few novelists can give you, power. I do not know a
novel in which the pain, the ecstasy, the ruthlessness, the
obsessiveness of love have been so wonderfully described. *Wuthering Heights* reminds me of one of those
great pictures of El Greco in which in a somber, arid land-
scape under dark clouds heavy with thunder, long, emaci-
ated figures in contorted attitudes, spellbound by an un-
earthly emotion, hold their breath. A streak of lightning
flitting across the leaden sky gives a final touch of mysterious terror to the scene.

GUSTAVE FLAUBERT

and

MADAME BOVARY

GUSTAVE FLAUBERT was a very unusual man. The French are of the opinion that he was a genius. But genius is a word loosely applied today: the Oxford English Dictionary describes it as an instinctive and extraordinary capacity for imaginative creation, original thought, invention, or discovery; and comparing it with talent, suggests that it achieves its results by instinctive perception and spontaneous activity rather than by processes which admit of being distinctly analyzed. By this standard no century is likely to produce more than three or four geniuses, and it is only to discredit the word to apply it to the composer of agreeable tunes, the writer of lively comedies or the painter of engaging pictures. They are very well in their way and their authors may have talent, which is a fine thing to have and a rare one; but genius is on another plane. If I were pressed to say what genius this twentieth century has produced I think that Albert Einstein is the only name that would occur to me. The nineteenth century was richer; but whether Flaubert can be counted among those who had this special gift the reader of this introduction, bearing in mind the dictionary's definition, may be able to decide for himself.

One thing admits of little doubt: Flaubert created the modern realistic novel and directly or indirectly has influenced all the writers of fiction since his day. Thomas Mann when he wrote *Buddenbrooks,* Arnold Bennett when he wrote *The Old Wives' Tale,* Theodore Dreiser when he wrote *Sister Carrie* were following a trail that Flaubert blazed. No writer that we know of devoted himself with such a fierce and indomitable industry to the art of literature. It was not with him as it is with most authors, an activity of paramount importance, but one that allows for other activities which rest the mind, refresh the body or enrich the experience. He did not think that to live was the object of life; for him the object of life was to write: no monk in his cell ever more willingly sacrificed the pleasures of the world to the love of God than Flaubert sacrificed the fullness and variety of life to his ambition to create a work of art.

The sort of books an author writes depends on the sort of man he is and that is why, if he is a good writer, it is well to know what is possible of his personal history. In the case of Flaubert this is peculiarly important. He was born at Rouen in 1821. His father was head of the hospital and lived there with his wife and children. It was a happy, highly respected and affluent family. Flaubert was brought up like any other French boy of his class; he went to school, he made friends with other boys, he worked little but read much. He was emotional and imaginative, and like many another child and boy was troubled by that sense of inner loneliness which the sensitive carry with them all their lives.

"I went to school when I was only ten," he wrote, "and I very soon contracted a profound aversion to the human race." That is not just a quip; he meant it. He was a pessimist from his youth up. It is true that just then romanticism was in full flower and pessimism was the fashion; one of the boys at Flaubert's school blew his brains out, another hanged himself with his necktie; but one cannot quite see why Flaubert, with a comfortable home, affectionate and indulgent parents, a doting sister and friends of whom he was passionately fond, should have really found life intolerable and his fellow creatures hateful. He was healthy, strong and well-grown. His early stories, written when he was a boy, are a hotchpotch of the worst extravagances of romanticism, and the pessimism with which they are imbued might reasonably be looked upon as merely a literary affectation. But Flaubert's was certainly not affected, nor was it attributable to foreign influence. He was pessimistic by nature, and if one asks why one must look into the abnormality of his physical constitution.

When he was fifteen an event took place that affected his whole life. His family went in the summer to Trouville, then a modest village by the sea with one hotel; and there that year they found staying Maurice Schlesinger, a music publisher and something of an adventurer, with his wife. It is worth while to transcribe the portrait Flaubert drew of her later: "She was tall, a brunette with magnificent black hair that fell in tresses to her shoulders; her nose was Greek, her eyes burning, her eyebrows high and admirably arched, her skin was glowing and as it were misty with gold; she was slender and exquisite, one saw the blue veins meandering on her brown and purple throat. Add to that a fine down that darkened her upper lip and gave her face a masculine and energetic expression such as to throw blonde beauties into the shade. She spoke slowly, her voice was modulated, musical and soft." I hesitate to translate *pourpré* with purple, which does not sound very alluring, but that *is* the translation, and I think Flaubert used it in recollection of Ronsard's most celebrated poem without considering the impression it would make when used to describe a lady's throat.

He fell madly in love with her. She was twenty-six and was nursing a baby. But Flaubert was timid and he would have been afraid even to speak to her if her husband had not been a jovial, hearty fellow with whom it was easy to make friends. Maurice Schlesinger took the boy riding with him and on one occasion the three of them went for a sail. Flaubert and Élisa Schlesinger sat side by side, their shoulders touching and her dress against his hand; she spoke in a low, sweet voice, but he was in such a turmoil that he could not remember a word she said. The summer came to an end, the Schlesingers left, the Flauberts went back to Rouen and Gustave to school. He had entered upon the great, the lasting passion of his life. Two years later he returned to Trouville and was told that she had been and gone. He was seventeen. It seemed to him then that he had been before too wrought-up really to love her; he loved her differently now, with a man's desire, and her absence only exacerbated his passion. When he got home he took up again a book he had started, *The Memoirs of a Madman,* and told the story of the summer when he fell in love with Élisa Schlesinger.

When he was nineteen, to reward him for having graduated, his father sent him with a certain Dr. Cloquet on a trip to the Pyrenees and Corsica. He was then full grown. His contemporaries have described him as a giant, but he was only five foot eight and in California or Texas they would call a man of that height a little fellow; he was thin and graceful; his black lashes veiled enormous, sea-green eyes and his long fine hair fell to his shoulders. A woman who knew him then said forty years later that he was as beautiful as a Greek god. On the way back from Corsica the travelers stopped at Marseilles and one morning, coming from a bathe, Flaubert noticed a woman sitting in the courtyard of the hotel. She was young, and her sensual languor was attractive. Flaubert addressed her and they got into conversation. She was called Eulalie Faucaud and was waiting to join her husband, an official, in French Guiana. Flaubert and Eulalie Faucaud passed that night together, a night according to his own account of that flaming passion which is as beautiful as the setting of the sun in the snow. He left Marseilles and never saw her again. It was his first experience of the kind, and it made a deep impression upon him.

Shortly after this episode he went to Paris to study law, not because he wanted to be a lawyer, but because he had to adopt some profession; but he was bored in Paris, bored by his law books, bored by the life of the university; and he despised his fellow students for their mediocrity, their poses and their bourgeois tastes. It was during this period that he wrote a novelette called *November* in which he described his brief adventure with Eulalie Faucaud. But he gave her the shining eyes with their high arched brows, the upper lip with its bluish down, the white round neck of Élisa Schlesinger.

He got in touch with the Schlesingers again by calling upon the publisher at his office. He invited Flaubert to one of the dinner parties he gave every Wednesday in his apartment. Élisa was as beautiful as ever. When last she had seen Flaubert he was a hobbledehoy, now he was a man, eager, passionate and handsome. It did not take her long to discover that he loved her. He was soon on terms of intimacy with husband and wife and dined regularly with them on Wednesdays. They went for little trips together. But Flaubert was as timid as ever, and for long he had not the courage to declare his love. When at last he did she was not angry, as he had feared she might be, but she refused to become his mistress. Her story was curious. When first Flaubert met her, in 1836, he thought, as did everyone else, that she was the wife of

Maurice Schlesinger; she was not; she was married to a
certain Émile Judée who had got into trouble, whereupon Schlesinger had come forward with the offer to provide money sufficient to save him from prosecution on
the condition that he left France and gave up his wife.
This he did, and Schlesinger and Élisa Judée lived together, there being at the time no divorce in France,
till Judée's death in 1840 enabled them to marry. It is
said that notwithstanding his absence and death Élisa
continued to love Émile Judée; and it may be that this
old love and a sense of loyalty to the man who had given
her a home and was the father of her child combined to
make her hesitate to accede to Flaubert's desires. But he
was ardent and at last persuaded her to come one day
to his apartment; he awaited her with feverish anxiety;
it seemed that at length he was going to be rewarded
for his long devotion. She never came.

Then, in 1844, once more an event occurred that was
to have momentous consequences to Flaubert. One dark
night he was driving back to Rouen with his brother from
a property of their mother's which they had been visiting.
His brother, nine years older than he, had adopted their
father's profession. Suddenly, without warning, Flaubert
"felt himself carried away in a torrent of flames and fell
like a stone to the floor of the trap." When he recovered
consciousness he was covered with blood; his brother
had carried him into a neighboring house and bled him.
He was taken to Rouen, where his father bled him again;
he was dosed with valerian and indigo, a seton was put
in his neck; he was forbidden to smoke, drink or eat
meat. He continued for some time to have fits of great
violence. He had visual and auditory symptoms, a con-
vulsion and then lost consciousness. Afterwards he was
exhausted and his nervous system was in a state of
frantic tension. A great deal of mystery has surrounded
this illness, and the doctors have discussed it from various points of view. Some have frankly said it was epilepsy, and that is what his friends thought it was; his
niece in her Recollections has passed the matter over in
silence; M. René Dumesnil, himself a doctor and the
author of an important work on Flaubert, claims that it
was not epilepsy, but what he calls hystero-epilepsy, I
think with the idea at the back of his mind that to ac-

knowledge that a distinguished writer was an epileptic somewhat took away from the value of his work.

It is possible that the attack did not come as a complete surprise to his family. He is reputed to have told Maupassant that he had first had auditory and visual hallucinations when he was twelve years old; when Flaubert was sent on a journey at the age of nineteen it was with a doctor and, since change of scene was part of the treatment his father afterwards prescribed, it does not seem unlikely that he had already had something in the nature of nervous attacks. Flaubert even as a boy had never felt himself quite like the people whom he came in contact with. Is it not possible that the curious pessimism of his early youth had its cause in the mysterious disease which must even then have been affecting his nervous system? Anyhow, he was faced now with the fact that he was afflicted with a terrifying malady, the attacks of which were unpredictable. It was necessary to change his mode of life. He decided, willingly enough it may be supposed, to abandon the law, and decided never to marry.

In 1845 his father died, and two months later his sister Caroline, whom he adored, after giving birth to a daughter, died also. As children they had been inseparable, and till her marriage she was his closest and dearest companion.

Some time before his death Dr. Flaubert had bought a property, called Croisset, on the banks of the Seine, with a fine stone house two hundred years old, a terrace in front of it and a little pavilion looking over the river. Here the widow settled with her son Gustave and the baby daughter of Caroline; her elder son, Achille, was married and, a surgeon like his father, succeeded him at the Rouen hospital. Croisset was to be Flaubert's home for the rest of his life. He had been writing off and on from a very early age and now, cut off as he was from living as most men live, he made up his mind to devote himself wholly to literature. He had a large workroom on the ground floor with windows on the river and the garden. He adopted methodical habits. He got up about ten, read his letters and the papers, lunched lightly at eleven and till one lounged about the terrace or sat in the pavilion reading. At one he set to work and worked till dinner at seven, then he took another stroll in the garden and went back to work till far into the night. He saw nobody but a friend or two whom now and then he invited to stay with him for a few days so that he might discuss his work with him. For the rest he denied himself any form of relaxation.

But he was aware that to write it was necessary to have experience of the world and that he could not afford to live entirely the life of a recluse. He made a point, therefore, of going to Paris for three or four months every year. In course of time, as he became well known, he made the acquaintance of the intellectuals of the day. I seem to gather that he was admired rather than liked. His companions found him very sensitive and very irritable. He would suffer no contradiction, and they took care not to disagree with him since if they ventured to do so his rage was alarming. He was a harsh critic of other men's work and shared a delusion common to authors that what he could not do himself was worthless. On the other hand he was infuriated by any criticism of his own work and ascribed it to jealousy, malice or stupidity. In this too he was not unlike many another distinguished author. He had no patience with the writers who wanted to earn their living by their pens or made any effort to advance themselves. He was of the opinion that the artist demeaned himself by making money. It was of course less difficult for him to take up this disinterested attitude since he had for the period a substantial fortune.

But this is somewhat to anticipate. In 1846, during one of his visits to Paris, he met in the studio of Pradier, the sculptor, a poetess called Louise Colet. Her husband, Hippolyte Colet was a professor of music; her lover, Victor Cousin, a philosopher. She was one of those writers, far from rare in the world of letters, who suppose that push and pull are an adequate substitute for talent; and with beauty to help she had acquired something of a position in literary circles. She had a salon frequented by celebrities and was known as the Muse. She wore her fair hair in ringlets that framed her round face; her voice was passionate, violent and tender. Within a month Flaubert became her lover, not of course displacing the philosopher, whose attachment to her was official; and when I say he became her lover it is in a manner of speaking, for to his mortification his excitement or his timidity made it for the time impossible for him to consummate the union. He returned to Croisset and wrote to Louise

Colet the first of a long series of as strange love letters as a lover can ever have written to his mistress. The Muse loved Flaubert, but she was exacting and jealous: he was neither. I think we may guess that he was proud to be the lover of a woman who was beautiful and very much in the public eye; but he was a man who lived a rich life of the imagination and like many another day-dreamer found that the realization fell sadly short of the anticipation. He discovered that he loved the Muse more when he was at Croisset than when he was in Paris, and he told her so. She wanted him to come and live in Paris; he told her that he could not leave his mother; then she asked him to come more often either to Paris or to Mantes, where on rare occasions they met; he told her he could only get away if he had a reasonable excuse, whereupon she answered angrily: "Does that mean that you're watched over like a girl?" She suggested coming to Croisset, but this he wouldn't let her do in any circumstances.

"Your love isn't love," she wrote. "In any case it doesn't mean much in your life." To this he replied: "You want to know if I love you? Well, yes, as much as I can love; that's to say, for me love isn't the first thing in life, but the second." He was really very tactless: he asked Louise Colet on one occasion to find out from a friend of hers who had lived at Cayenne what had happened to Eulalie Faucaud, the object of his adventure at Marseilles, and even asked her to have a letter delivered to her; he was astonished that she accepted the commission with some show of irritation. He went so far as to tell her of his encounters with prostitutes for whom he had, according to his own story, an inclination which he frequently gratified. But there is nothing men lie about so much as their sex life, and I ask myself whether here he was not boasting of a virility which he somewhat lacked. No one knows how often he had the fits that left him weak and depressed, but he was constantly under the influence of sedatives, and it may well be that he consented to see Louise Colet so seldom—remember he was then in his twenties—because his sexual desires were not pressing.

The affair, such as it was, lasted for nine months. In 1849 Flaubert started for the near East with Maxime du Camp. The two friends visited Egypt, Palestine, Syria and Greece, and in the spring of 1851 returned to France. Flaubert resumed relations with Louise Colet, and as before engaged in an increasingly acrimonious correspondence. She continued to press him to come to Paris or to let her come to Croisset; he continued to find reasons not to do the one nor to allow her to do the other; and in the end, in 1854, he wrote to tell her that he would not see her again. She hurried to Croisset and was roughly turned away. This was Flaubert's last serious affair. There had been more literature than life in it, more playacting than passion. The only woman Flaubert sincerely and devotedly loved in his life was Élisa Schlesinger. Her husband's speculations had ended in disaster, and the Schlesingers had gone with their children to live in Baden. Flaubert did not see Élisa again for twenty years. By that time both were much changed. She was thin, her skin had lost its delicate hues and her hair was white; he had grown corpulent, he had an immense moustache and to conceal his baldness he wore a black cap. They met, they parted. In 1871 Maurice Schlesinger died, and Flaubert, after loving her for thirty-five years, wrote his first love letter to her: instead of beginning as he always had done, Dear Madame, he began, "My old love, my ever loved one." She had to come to France on business. They met at Croisset, they met in Paris. After that, so far as anyone knows, they never met again.

During his journey in the East, Flaubert had been turning over in his mind the idea of a novel which was to be for him an entirely new departure. This was *Madame Bovery*. How he came to write it makes a curious story. On a trip to Italy he had seen at Genoa a picture by Brueghel of the Temptation of St. Anthony which greatly impressed him, and on his return to France he bought an engraving by Callot of the same subject. He then set about reading all the relevant material, and when he had acquired the information he required he wrote the book which these two pictures had suggested to him. Having finished it, he sent for his two most intimate friends to come to Croisset to hear him read it. He read for four days, for four hours in the afternoon and for four hours at night. It was arranged that no opinion should be given till the whole work had been heard. At midnight on the fourth day Flaubert, having read to the end, banged his fist on the table said: "Well?"

One of them answered: "We think you ought to throw it in the fire and not speak of it again." It was a shattering blow. Next day the same friend, looking for some way to soften it, said to Flaubert: "Why don't you write the story of Delamare?" Flaubert gave a start, his face lit up and he said: "Why not?" Delamare had been an interne at the hospital at Rouen and his story was well known. He had a practice in a small town near Rouen, and after the death of his first wife, a widow much older than himself, he married the pretty young daughter of a neighboring farmer. She was pretentious and extravagant. She quickly grew bored with her dull husband and took a series of lovers. She spent on clothes money she could not afford and ran hopelessly into debt. Finally she took poison. Flaubert followed this mean little story with complete fidelity.

He was thirty when he began to write *Madame Bovary*. He had published nothing. With the exception of *The Temptation of St. Anthony* the more important of his early works had been strictly personal; they were in fact novelizations of his amorous experiences. His aim now was to be not only realistic, but objective. He determined to tell the truth without bias or prejudice, and not in any way himself to enter into the narrative. He determined to put the facts he had to tell and expose the characters of the persons he had to deal with without comment of his own, neither condemning nor praising; if he sympathized with one, not to show it; if the stupidity of another exasperated him, the malice of a third outraged him, not to allow a word of his to reveal it. This is what he did, and that perhaps is why many readers have found a certain coldness in the novel. There is nothing heart-warming in this calculated, obstinate detachment. Though it may be a weakness in us, my impression is that as readers we find a comfort in knowing that the author shares the emotions he has made us feel.

But the attempt at complete impersonality fails with Flaubert as it fails with every novelist, because complete impersonality is impossible. It is very well that the novelist should let his characters explain themselves and as far as may be let their actions be the outcome of their characters, and the author may easily make a nuisance of himself when he draws your attention to his heroine's charm or his villain's malevolence, when he moralizes or irrelevantly digresses, when in fact he is himself a personage in the story he is telling; but this is only a matter of method, a method that some very good novelists have used, and if it happens to have gone out of fashion at the moment that is not to say it is a bad one. But the author who avoids it keeps his personality only out of the surface of his novel; he reveals it willy-nilly by his choice of subject, his choice of characters and the point of view from which he describes them. Flaubert as we know was a pessimist. He had no patience with stupidity. The bourgeois, the commonplace, the ordinary filled him with exasperation. He had no pity. He had no charity. All his adult life he was a sick man oppressed by the humiliation with which his disease filled him. His nerves were in a constant state of perturbation. He was violently intolerant. He was a romantic who feared his romanticism. He flung himself into the sordid story of Madame Bovary with the zest of a man revenging himself on life by wallowing in the gutter, because life has not met the demands of his passion for the ideal. He did not keep his personality out of his novel when he decided to write the story of Delamare, nor when he constructed the characters who were to take part in it. We are introduced to many persons in the course of the novel's five hundred pages, and with the exception of Dr. Larivière, a minor character, not one has a redeeming feature. They are base, mean, stupid, trivial and vulgar. A great many people are, but not all; and it is inconceivable that in a town, however small, there should not be found one person at least, if not two or three, who was sensible, kindly and helpful.

Flaubert's deliberate intention was to choose a set of characters who were thoroughly commonplace, and devise incidents that would inevitably arise from their nature and their circumstances; but he was faced with the possibility that no one would be interested in persons so dull and that the incidents he had to relate would prove tedious. How he proposed to deal with this I will come to later. Before doing so I want to consider how far he succeeded in his attempt.

First I want to point out that the characters are drawn with consummate skill. We are persuaded of their truth. We no sooner meet them than we accept them as living creatures, standing on their own feet, in the world we know. We take them for granted as we take our plumber, our grocer, our doctor. It never occurs to us that they are figures in a novel. Homais, to mention one, is a creature as humorous as Mr. Micawber. He has become as familiar to the French as Mr. Micawber is to the English. We believe in him as we can never quite believe in Mr. Micawber, and unlike Mr. Micawber he is always consistently himself.

But I cannot persuade myself that Emma Bovary is the ordinary farmer's daughter. That there was in her something of every woman and of every man is true. When Flaubert was asked who was the model for her he said: Madame Bovary is me. We are all given to extravagant and absurd reveries in which we see ourselves rich, handsome, successful, the heroes or heroines of romantic adventures, but most of us are too sensible, too timorous or too unadventurous to let our reveries seriously affect our behavior. Madame Bovary was exceptional in that she tried to live her dream-life; she was exceptional in her beauty. Nor have the incidents quite the inevitability that Flaubert sought. When Emma Bovary is let down by her first lover she has an attack of brain fever that brings her to death's door and lasts for forty-three days. Now brain fever, for long a favorite illness with novelists who wanted to dispose for a while of a character, is not, I understand, a malady known to the medical profession; and if Flaubert let her suffer from it in so severe a form, I suspect it was only because he wanted her to have a long and expensive illness. The episode does not enforce belief; nor, for the matter of that, does Bovary's death: he dies merely because Flaubert wanted to finish his book.

As is well known author and publisher were prosecuted on the charge that *Madame Bovary* was an immoral work: I have read the speeches of the public prosecutor and of the defending counsel. The prosecutor read a number of passages which he claimed were pornographic; they make one smile now, they are so decent in comparison with the descriptions of the act of love to which modern novelists have accustomed us; but one cannot believe that even then (in 1857) the prosecutor was shocked by them. The defending counsel pleaded that these passages were necessary, and that the moral of the novel was good because Madame Bovary suffered for her misbehavior. The judges accepted his view and the defendants were acquitted. It does not seem to have occurred to anyone at the time that if Madame Bovary came to a bad end it was not because she committed adultery, but because she ran up bills that she hadn't the money to pay for. If she had had the economical instincts of the French peasant that we are told she was, there is no reason why she should not have gone from lover to lover without coming to harm.

I hope the reader will not think that I am tiresomely finding trivial faults in a great book; the point I want to make is that Flaubert did not quite succeed in doing what he was attempting because he was attempting the impossible. A work of fiction is an arrangement of incidents devised to display a number of characters in action and to interest the reader. It is not a copy of life as it is lived. Just as in a novel conversations cannot be reproduced exactly as they take place in real life, but have to be summarized so that only the essential points are given, and then with a clearness and concision which is not found in real life, so facts have to suffer some deformation in order to conform with the author's plan and to hold the reader's attention. Irrelevant incidents must be omitted; repetitions must be avoided, and heaven knows, life is full of repetitions; unrelated occurrences and events that may in real life be separated by a period of time may often have to be brought into proximity. No novel is entirely free of improbabilities, and to the more usual ones indeed readers have become so used that they accept them as a matter of course. The novelist cannot give a literal transcript of life, he draws a picture for you which, if he is a realist, he tries to make lifelike; and if you believe him he has succeeded.

Flaubert has succeeded. *Madame Bovary* gives an impression of intense reality, and this, I think, arises not only because his characters are eminently lifelike, but because, with his peculiar acuity of observation, he has described every detail essential to this purpose with extraordinary accuracy. The book is very well constructed. Some critics have found it a fault that though Emma is the central character it begins with a description of Bovary's early youth and first marriage and finishes with his disentegration and death. I think Flaubert's idea was to enclose the story of Emma within the story of her husband as you enclose a painting in a frame. He must have felt that, I believe, so he rounded off his narrative and gave it the unity of a work of art. If this was his intention it would have been more evident if the end were not hurried and arbitrary.

There is one part of the book which I have not seen mentioned by the critics, but to which I should like to draw the reader's attention since it is an admirable example of Flaubert's skill in composition. The first months of Emma's married life were passed in the village called Tostes, she was immensely bored there, but for the balance of the book this period had to be described at the same pace and with the same detail as the rest. Now it is very difficult to describe a boring time without boring the reader, yet you read this long passage with interest; I was curious to see how it had been done and read it over again. I discovered that Flaubert had narrated a long series of very trivial incidents, each one new, none repeated; and you are not bored because you are reading something fresh all the time; but because each little incident is so commonplace, so lacking in excitement, you do get a vivid, even a devastating, sensation of Emma's boredom. There is a set piece of description of Yonville, the little town in which the Bovarys settled after leaving Tostes, but it is the only one; for the rest of the descriptions of country or town, beautifully done all of them, are interwoven with the narrative. They serve the purpose, which all such descriptions should serve, of getting on with the story. Flaubert introduces his persons in action and we learn of their appearance, their mode of living, their setting in a continuous process, as in fact we come to know people in real life.

I remarked a few pages back that Flaubert was conscious that in setting out to write a novel about commonplace people he ran the risk of writing a very dull one. He was determined to produce a work of art and he felt that he could surmount the difficulties presented by the sordid nature of his subject and the vulgarity of his characters only by means of beauty of style. Now I don't know if such a creature exists as the natural-born stylist; certainly Flaubert was not one. His early works, unpublished in his lifetime, appear to be verbose and rhetorical, and his letters, written in a faulty French, show little sign that he had a feeling for the elegance and distinction of his native tongue. With *Madame Bovary* he made himself one of the greatest stylists in France. This is a matter upon which a foreigner, even if he knows a language well, can be but an uncertain judge; the finer points can hardly fail to escape him, and obviously in a translation the music, the subtlety, the aptness, the rhythm of the original must be lost. All the same it seems to me worth while to tell the reader what Flaubert was aiming at and how he set about achieving his aim, for much can be learned from his theory and practice that will be useful to the writer of any country.

Flaubert adopted as his own the maxim of Buffon that to write well, one must at the same time feel well, think well and say well. He was of the opinion that there were not two ways of saying a thing, but only one, and that the wording must fit the thought as the glove fits the hand. His desire was to write a prose that was logical, precise, swift and various. He wished to make it as rhythmical, sonorous and musical as poetry, and yet preserve the qualities of prose. He was prepared to use the words of everyday life, vulgarisms if need be, so long as he could so use them as to produce an effect of beauty.

Now all this is surely admirable. One may be permitted to think that sometimes he went too far. "When I find a dissonance or a repetition in one of my phrases," he said, "I know that I'm ensnared in something false." He would not allow himself to use the same word twice on a page. That seems absurd; if it is the right word in each place it is the right word to use and a synonym or a periphrase can never be as good. He was careful not to allow his sense of rhythm to obsess him (as George Moore in his later works was obsessed) but took pains to vary it. He had a peculiar skill in combining words and sounds to give an impression of speed or languor, of lassitude or intensity, in fact of whatever state he desired to represent. I have not space here, even if I had the knowledge, to enlarge further on the particular qualities of Flaubert's style, but I should like to say a few words about how he became the master he did.

First of all he worked hard. Before starting on a book he read everything he could find that was pertinent. He made voluminous notes. When writing he would sketch out roughly what he wished to say and then work on what he had written, elaborating, cutting, rewriting, till

he got the effect he wanted. That done, he would go out
onto his terrace and shout out the phrases he had written, convinced that if they did not sound well to the ear,
if by their form they were not perfectly easy to say,
there must be something wrong with them. In that case
he would take them back and work over them again
until he was at last satisfied. In one of his letters he
writes: "The whole of Monday and Tuesday were taken
up with a search for two lines." This of course does
not mean that he wrote only two lines in two days, he
may well have written ten or a dozen pages; it means that
with all that labor he succeeded in writing only two
lines as perfect as he wanted them. It is no wonder that
Madame Bovary took him fifty-five months to write.

I have little more to say. After *Madame Bovary* he
wrote *Salammbô*, which is generally considered a failure, then he wrote another version of *The Sentimental
Education,* a novel he had written many years before and
had been dissatisfied with, in which he again described
his love for Élisa Schlesinger. It is by many good critics
in France looked upon as his masterpiece. A foreigner
must find it hard to read because great sections of it are
concerned with matters that today can be of no interest
to him. After this, for the third time, he wrote *The
Temptation of St. Anthony*. It is curious to note that so
great a writer should have had so few ideas for books
which he developed sufficiently to write. He was apparently content to take up again and again the subjects
that obsessed his youth: it is as though he could not
disembarrass his soul of the burden of them until he
had written them down in a definite form.

Time passed and his niece Caroline married. Flaubert
and his mother were left alone. His mother died. After
the defeat of France in 1870 his niece's husband found
himself in financial difficulties and finally, to save him
from bankruptcy, Flaubert handed over to him his whole
fortune. He kept for himself only the old home he
could not bear to part with. As long as he was affluent he
had held money in some contempt, but when by his own
disinterested act he was reduced to comparative poverty
the worry brought on again the fits from which for a
decade he had been almost free and then, whenever he
was in Paris and went out to dinner, Guy de Maupassant
went to fetch him and see him safely home. Though on

the whole unfortunate in his love affairs, he had always had a few devoted, loyal and affectionate friends. One by one most of them died and his last years were lonely. He seldom left Croisset. He smoked too much. He drank too much apple brandy.

The last work he published was a volume of three stories. He engaged upon a novel called *Buvard et Pécuchet* in which he determined to have his final fling at the stupidity of the human race, and with his usual thoroughness he read fifteen hundred books to provide himself with the material he thought necessary. It was to be in two volumes, and he almost reached the end of the first. On the morning of May 8, 1880, the maid went into the library at eleven to bring him his lunch. She found him lying on the divan muttering incomprehensible words. She ran for the doctor and brought him back with her. He could do nothing. In less than an hour Gustave Flaubert was dead. . . .

A year later his old friend, Maxime du Camp, spent the summer in Baden, and one day when he was out hunting found himself near the lunatic asylum of Illenau. The gates opened to allow the inmates to take their daily walk, and they came out two by two. Among them was one who bowed to him. It was Élisa Schlesinger, the woman whom Flaubert had so long and so vainly loved.

CHARLES DICKENS

and

DAVID COPPERFIELD

CHARLES DICKENS, though small, was of a pleasing appearance. There is a portrait of him painted by Maclise when he was twenty-seven, which is in the National Portrait Gallery in London. He is seated in a very grand chair at a writing table, with a small, elegant hand just resting on a manuscript. He is smartly dressed and wears a vast satin neckcloth. His brown hair is curled and falls luxuriantly down each side of his face well below the ears. His face is long and pale, his eyes fine; and the thoughtful expression he wears is such as an admiring public might expect of a successful young author. He was always something of a dandy and in his youth favored velvet coats, gay vests, colored neckcloths and white hats, but he never quite achieved the effect he sought; people were surprised and even shocked by his dress, which they described as both slipshod and flashy.

His grandfather, William Dickens, began life as a footman, married a housemaid and eventually became steward at Crewe Hall, the seat of John Crewe, Member of Parliament for Chester. He had two sons, William and John, but the only one that concerns us is John, first because he was the father of England's greatest novelist, and second because he served as model for his son's greatest creation, Mr. Micawber. William the elder died when John was born, and his widow stayed on at Crewe Hall for thirty-five years as housekeeper. She was then pensioned. The Crewes educated the two sons and provided them with a means of livelihood. They got John a post in the Navy Pay Office, where he made friends with a fellow clerk and presently married his sister Elizabeth Barrow. John Dickens is described as an old buck who dressed well and was forever fingering the large bunch of seals attached to his watch. He seems to have had a taste for good wine, since the second time he was arrested for debt it was at the suit of a firm of wine merchants. From the very beginning of his married life he appears to have been in financial trouble and he was always ready to borrow money from anyone who was unwise enough to lend it to him.

Charles, the second child of John and Elizabeth Dickens, was born in 1812 at Portsea, but two years later his father was transferred to London and three years after that to Chatham. There the boy was put to school and there he began to read. His father had a small collection of books, *Tom Jones, The Vicar of Wakefield, Gil Blas, Don Quixote, Roderick Random* and *Peregrine Pickle;* Charles read and re-read them, and his own novels show how great an influence they had on him.

In 1822 John Dickens, who by this time had five children, was moved back to London; but Charles was left at Chatham to continue his schooling and did not rejoin his family for some months. They were then settled in Camden Town on the outskirts of the city in a house which he was later to describe as the home of the Micawbers. John Dickens, though earning a little more than three hundreds pounds a year (which would be equivalent today to something like five thousand dollars), was apparently in more than usually desperate straits, and it would seem that there was not enough money to send little Charles to school again. To his disgust he was put to minding the children, cleaning the boots, brushing the clothes and doing the housework. But in the intervals he roamed about Camden Town, "a desolate place surrounded by fields and ditches" and the neighboring Somers Town and Kentish Town; and later, going further, he came to know Soho and Limehouse.

Things were so bad with the family that Mrs. Dickens decided to open a school for the children of parents living in India; she borrowed money to rent a house and had handbills printed for distribution, which the children were sent to push into the letter boxes in the neighborhood; but not a single pupil came. Debts were pressing, and Charles was sent to pawn everything on which a little cash could be raised; the books, the precious books which meant so much to him, were sold to a bookseller. Then James Lamert, a stepson of Mrs. Dickens' sister, offered Charles a job at six or seven shillings a week in a blacking factory of which he was part owner. His parents thankfully accepted the offer; it reduced Charles to despair. It cut him to the quick that they should be so manifestly relieved to get him off their hands. He was twelve years old, quick, eager and intelligent, and he felt "a deep sense of abandonment."

Shortly afterwards the long awaited blow fell. John Dickens was arrested for debt and taken to the Marshalsea; and there his wife, after pawning the little that was left to pawn, joined him with her children. The Marshalsea and the Fleet were the two London prisons for debt. They were filthy, unsanitary and crowded, for not only were they occupied by the prisoners, but by the families they might, if they chose, bring with them; though whether they were allowed to do this to alleviate the hardships of prison life or because the unfortunate creatures had nowhere else to go, I do not know. If a debtor had money, loss of liberty was the worst of the inconveniences he had to endure, and this loss in some cases might be mitigated: particular prisoners were permitted, on observing certain conditions, to reside outside the prison walls. But if the debtor was penniless it went ill with him. It may interest American readers to know that it was General Oglethorpe who first made an effort to improve the shocking conditions that he found prevailing. It appears that a friend of his was imprisoned, and not having the money to pay the warden's fees, was placed in a house in which smallpox was raging; he caught the disease and died. General Oglethorpe succeeded in inducing Parliament to conduct an inquiry, which revealed that the warden was in the habit of practicing outrageous extortion on the prisoners and often treated them with barbarous cruelty. The worst abuses were done away with, and by the time John Dickens was consigned to prison he was able to make himself sufficiently comfortable. Mrs. Dickens brought a little maid with her, who lived out, but came in daily to help with the children and prepare the family meals. John Dickens still had his salary of six pounds a week, but made no attempt to pay his debt, and it may be supposed that, content to be out of reach of his other creditors, he did not particularly care to be released. The biographers have been puzzled by the fact that he continued in these circumstances to receive his wage. The only explanation appears to be that as government clerks were appointed by influence, such an accident as being imprisoned for debt was not considered so grave a matter as to call for so drastic a step as cutting off a salary. It may be also that it was paid by some other department than that which enjoyed the services of John Dickens and this department never discovered that he was not doing the work for which he was being paid.

At the beginning of his father's imprisonment Charles lodged in Camden Town; but since this was a long way from the blacking factory, which was at Hungerford Stairs, Charing Cross, he moved to Southwark and was then able to breakfast and sup with his family in the Marshalsea. The work was not hard; it consisted in washing the bottles, labeling them and tying them up. In the evenings he wandered about London, finding his way to strange and mysterious places about Thamesside, and thus insensibly absorbed a sense of the romance of the great city which he never afterwards lost. In April 1824 Mrs. William Dickens, the Crewe's old housekeeper, died and left her small savings to her two sons. John Dickens' debt was paid (by his brother) and he regained his freedom. He settled his family once more in Camden Town and went back to work at the Navy Pay Office. Charles continued to wash bottles at the factory for a while, but then owing to something John Dickens wrote to James Lamert, he was fired. He went home "with a relief so great that it was like oppression," he wrote many years later: his mother tried to smooth things down so that Charles should retain his job and the six shillings a week of his wages, which she doubtless needed; and for this he never forgave her. "I never afterwards forgot, I never shall forget, I never can forget that my mother was warm for my being sent back," he added. John Dickens would not hear of it and sent his son to school.

It is difficult to make out how long the boy spent at the blacking factory: he went there early in February 1824 and was back with his family by June, so that at the outside he cannot have been at the factory more than four months. Dame Una Pope-Hennessy in her excellent book on Charles Dickens states that he was there no more than six weeks. It made, however, a deep impression on him, and he looked upon the experience as so humiliating that he could not bear to speak of it. When John Forster, his biographer, by chance hit upon some inkling of it, Dickens told him that he had touched upon a matter so painful that "even at the present hour," and this was twenty-five years later, "he could never lose the remembrance of it while he remembered anything."

We are so used to hearing eminent politicians and captains of industry boast of having in their youth washed dishes or sold newspapers that it is hard for us to understand why Charles Dickens should have worked himself up into looking upon it as a great injury that his parents had done him when they sent him to the blacking factory and a secret so shameful that it must be concealed. He was a merry, mischievous, alert boy, and, one would have thought, already knew something of the seamy side of life. His parents were of humble extraction, and from a very early age he had seen to what a pass his father's improvidence reduced the family. At Camden Town he was put to sweep and scrub; he was sent to pawn articles to buy food for dinner; and like any other boy he must have played in the streets with boys of the same sort as himself. It is hard to see why he should have found it such a degradation to consort with the other boys who were working in the blacking factory. A lad of that age surely has little sense of social distinctions. My own surmise is that he did not suffer as much as in after years, when he was famous and respectable, a social as well as a public figure, he persuaded himself he had. He lived at a time when to follow a "menial occupation" was derogatory and he had been too often accused of vulgarity not to be sensitive about his antecedents. It was a period when to be a gentleman was to be one of God's chosen creatures.

While still in the Marshalsea John Dickens had had the nerve to solicit the head of the department which employed him to recommend him for a superannuation grant on the ground of his ill health; and eventually, in consideration of his twenty years' service and six children, he was granted, "on compassionate grounds," a pension of one hundred and forty-five pounds a year. This was little enough on which to support a family and he had to find some means of adding to his income. He had acquired a knowledge of shorthand, possibly, Dame

Una suggests, while in prison; and with the help of his brother-in-law, who had press connections, he got a job as a parliamentary reporter. Charles remained at school till he was fifteen when he went to work as an errand boy in a lawyer's office; he was there for a few weeks, after which his father managed to get him engaged as a clerk in another lawyer's office at fifteen shillings a week. In his spare time he learned shorthand, and in eighteen months was sufficiently competent to set up as a reporter in the Consistory Court of Doctors' Commons. By the time he was twenty he had qualified as a parliamentary reporter, and joined the staff of a paper to report the speeches made in the House of Commons. He gained the reputation of being "the fastest and most accurate man in the Gallery."

Meanwhile he had fallen in love with Maria Beadnell, the daughter of a bank manager; she was a flirtatious young person, and she seems to have given him a good deal of encouragement. There may even have been a secret engagement between them, but if there was she did not take it seriously. She was flattered and amused to have a lover, but Charles was penniless and she never can have intended to marry him. When after two years the affair came to an end, and in true romantic fashion they returned one another's presents, Charles thought his heart would break. After he had written *David Copperfield,* in which she appeared as Dora, a woman friend once asked him whether he had really loved her "so very, very very much"; he answered that there was "no woman in the world and few men who could realize how much." They did not meet again till many years later when Maria Beadnell, long a married woman, dined with the celebrated Mr. Dickens and his wife: she was fat, commonplace and stupid. She served then as the model for Flora Finching in *Little Dorrit.*

At the age of twenty-two Charles Dickens was earning five guineas a week. In order to be near the office of his paper he took lodgings in one of the dingy streets off the Strand, but finding them unsatisfactory he rented unfurnished rooms in Furnival's Inn. But before he could furnish them his father was again arrested for debt, and he had to provide money for his keep at the sponging house. Since he was likely to be detained for some time Charles took cheap lodgings for the family, and camped out with his brother Frederick, whom he took charge of, in the "three-pair-back" at Furnival's Inn. "Just because he was open-hearted as well as open-handed and seemed able to deal with difficulties of the kind easily, it became the custom in his own family, and later on in his wife's family, to expect him to find money and appointments for as spineless a set of people as ever breadwinner was saddled with." *

When he had been working for a year or so in the Gallery of the House of Commons, Dickens began to write a series of sketches of London life; the first were published in the *Monthly Magazine* and later ones in the *Morning Chronicle;* he was paid nothing for them, but they attracted attention. There was a vogue at the time for anecdotal novels of a humorous character, which were issued in monthly parts at a shilling with comic illustrations, and distinguished writers were engaged by the publishers to provide the letterpress. They were the remote ancestors of the funnies of our own day and they had the same prodigious popularity. One day a partner in the firm of Chapman and Hall called upon Dickens to ask him to write a narrative about a club of amateur sportsmen to serve as a vehicle for the illustrations of a well-known artist. He offered fourteen pounds a month and additional payment on sales. Dickens protested that he knew nothing about sport and did not think he could write to order, but "the emolument was too tempting to resist." I need hardly say that the result was *The Posthumous Papers of the Pickwick Club:* never can another masterpiece have been written under such conditions. The first five numbers had no great success, but with the introduction of Sam Weller the circulation leaped up. By the time the work appeared in book form Charles Dickens, being then twenty-five, was famous. Though the critics had their reservations, his reputation was made. It is well to record that the *Quarterly Review,* speaking of him, said that "it required no gift of prophecy to foretell his fate—he has risen like a rocket and he will come down like a stick." But indeed, throughout his career, while the public devoured his books, the critics carped. Such is the shallowness of contemporary criticism.

* Una Pope-Hennessy. *Charles Dickens.*

A couple of days before the appearance of the first number of *The Pickwick Papers,* in 1836, Charles Dickens married Kate, the eldest daughter of George Hogarth, a colleague on the paper for which he was then working. George Hogarth was the father of six sons and eight daughters. The daughters were small, plump, fresh-colored and blue-eyed. Kate was the only one of marriageable age. That seems to have been the reason why he married her rather than one of the others. After a short honeymoon they settled down in Furnival's Inn and invited Kate's pretty sister, Mary Hogarth, a girl of six-teen, to live with them. Charles became attached to her and when Kate found herself with child and so could not go about with him, Mary was his constant companion. He had accepted a contract to write another novel, *Oliver Twist,* and started it while he was still at work on *The Pickwick Papers.* This also was to appear in monthly numbers and he devoted a fortnight to one and a fort-night to the other. Most novelists are so absorbed in the characters which are at the moment engaging their at-tention that, by no effort of will, they thrust back into their unconscious what other literary ideas they have had in mind; and that Dickens should have been able to switch, apparently with ease, from one story to another is an extraordinary feat.

Kate's baby was born, and as she might be expected to have several more a move was made from Furnival's Inn to a house in Doughty Street. Mary grew every day more lovely and more delightful. One May evening Dickens took Kate and Mary to a play; they enjoyed themselves and came home in high spirits. Mary was suddenly taken ill. A doctor was sent for. In a few hours she was dead. Dickens took the ring from her finger and put it on his own. He wore it till his death. He was prostrate with grief. Not very long after he wrote in his diary: "If she were with us now, the same winning, happy, amiable companion, sympathizing with all my thoughts and feel-ings more than anyone I know ever did or will, I think I should have nothing to wish for but a continuance of such happiness. But she is gone, and pray God I may one day, through His mercy, rejoin her." He arranged to be buried by her side.

The shock of Mary's death resulted in Kate's having a miscarriage, and when she was well enough Charles took her for a short trip abroad so that they might both recover their spirits. By the summer he at all events had sufficiently done so to have a boisterous flirtation with a certain Eleanor P.

The life of a literary man who has achieved success is not as a rule interesting. It follows a uniform pattern. His profession obliges him to devote a certain number of hours a day to his work, and he discovers a routine to suit him. He is brought into contact with the celebrated people of the day, literary, artistic and polite. He is taken up by great ladies. He goes to parties and gives parties. He travels. He makes public appearances. This, broadly, was the pattern of Dickens' life. He enjoyed a success such as has been the fortune of few authors to experience. He had always been fascinated by the theater, and, indeed, at one time had seriously thought of going on the stage; he learned parts by heart, took lessons in elocution from an actor, and practiced before a mirror how to enter a room, sit down on a chair and make a bow. These accomplishments were useful to him when he was introduced into the world of fashion. The censorious thought him faintly vulgar and his mode of dress flashy, but he charmed by his good looks, the brightness of his eyes, his exuberance, vivacity and joyous laugh. He was dazzled by the adulation of which he was the object, but his head was not turned. He remained modest.

Oddly enough, though he had an immense power of observation and in course of time came to be on familiar terms with persons in the higher ranks of society, he never succeeded in his novels in making such characters as he created in those walks of life quite credible. Nor are his parsons and doctors ever so lifelike as the lawyers and lawyer's clerks whom he had known when he worked in an office and as a reporter at Doctors' Commons, or as the underprivileged among whom his boyhood was spent. It looks as though a novelist can know intimately enough to use them profitably as models for creatures of his own invention only the persons with whom he has been connected at an early age. A child's year, a boy's year, is much, much longer than the year of a grown-up man, and he is thus given what seems like all the time in the world to make himself aware of the idiosyncrasies of the people who form his environment.

He gets to know them from the inside, whereas later he gets to know them only from the outside, and so misses that something by means of which he can make living persons of them. It is a disadvantage of success that it may well bring the author into a world other than his own, a world he can never know as can those who have been born and bred in it, and cut him off from his own world and so his truest source of inspiration. Dickens was fortunate in that owing to the crowded experience of his early years he could always single out from the men and women he came across in after life those whom he could put to literary use in his own characteristic way.

He was a hard worker and for several years started to write a new book long before he was finished with the old one. He wrote to please and kept his eye on the public reaction to the monthly numbers in which most of his novels appeared, and it is interesting to learn that he had no intention of sending Martin Chuzzlewit to America till the declining sales showed that the numbers were not as attractive as usual. He was not the sort of author who looks upon popularity as something to be ashamed of. The labor his great production entailed did not exhaust Dickens' energy. During the course of his life he founded and edited three weekly magazines. He played as hard as he worked. He thought nothing of walking twenty miles a day, he rode, he danced and played the fool with gusto, he did conjuring tricks to amuse his children, he acted in amateur theatricals; he attended banquets, he delivered lectures; he entertained lavishly.

As soon as circumstances permitted, the Dickenses moved into a new house in a more fashionable neighborhood and ordered from firms of repute complete suites for the reception rooms and bedrooms. Thick pile carpets were laid on the floors and festooned curtains adorned the windows. They engaged a good cook, three other maids and a man servant. They set up a carriage. They gave dinner parties to which noble and distinguished persons came. The profusion somewhat shocked the wife of Thomas Carlyle, and Lord Jeffrey wrote to his friend Lord Cockburn that he had dined in the new house and had "a rather too sumptuous dinner for a man with a family and only beginning to be rich." All this cost money, but he had other expenses besides: his father and his father's family, all of whom he supported, continued to be a drain on him. Among things the old buck did to embarrass his celebrated son was to borrow money on the strength of his success and sell his autographs and pages of his manuscripts. Dickens came to the conclusion that he would have no peace till he got the whole lot of them out of London; so, much to their disgust, he took a house for them at Alphington, near Exeter, and settled them there. It was partly to meet his heavy expenses that he founded the first of his magazines, *Master Humphrey's Clock,* and to give it a good send-off he published *The Old Curiosity Shop* in it. Its success was immense. David O'Connell, Sara Coleridge, Lord Jeffrey, Carlyle were overcome by its pathos. Crowds gathered on the quay at New York shouting to an incoming ship: "Is Little Nell dead?"

In 1842 Mr. and Mrs. Dickens, leaving their four children in the care of Georgina Hogarth, Kate's sister, went to America. Charles Dickens was lionized as no author has ever been before or since. But the trip was not a complete success. A hundred years ago the people of the United States, though ready enough to disparage things European, were exceedingly sensitive of any criticism of themselves. A hundred years ago the press of the United States was ruthless in its invasion of the privacy of any hapless person who was "news." A hundred years ago in the United States the publicity-minded looked upon the distinguished foreigner as a God-given opportunity and called him conceited when he showed a disinclination to be treated like a monkey in a zoo. A hundred years ago the United States was a land where speech was free so long as it did not offend the susceptibilities or affect the interests of other people, and where everyone was entitled to his own opinions so long as they agreed with those of everyone else. Of all this Charles Dickens was ignorant, and he made bad blunders. The absence of an International Copyright not only deprived English authors of any profit in the United States from the sale of their books ("It is but fair," said Washington Irving, "that those who have laurels for their brows should be permitted to browse on their laurels.") but also greatly hurt American authors, for the booksellers very naturally preferred to publish books by English authors which they could get for nothing rather than books by American authors for which they had to pay. But it was certainly tactless of Charles Dickens to introduce the subject in the speeches he made at the banquets given for him on his arrival. The reaction was violent and the newspapers described him as "no gentleman, but a mercenary scoundrel." Though he was mobbed by admirers, and at Philadelphia shook hands for two hours with the crowd who wanted to meet the great man; though souvenir hunters tore bits of fur out of his new fur coat, his personal success was not complete: it is true that most people were charmed by his youth, good looks and gaiety, but a good many found his appearance effeminate, his dress, his rings and diamond pins vulgar, and his manner lacking in refinement. But he made some good friends with whom he maintained an affectionate relation to his death.

The Dickenses returned to England after four eventful but exhausting months. The children had grown attached to their Aunt Georgina and the tired travelers asked her to make their home with them. She was sixteen, the age of Mary when she went to live at Furnival's Inn, and so like her that from a distance she might have been taken for her. Kate Dickens was expecting another baby. Georgy Hogarth was pretty, attractive and unassuming; she had a gift for mimicry by means of which she could make Dickens roar with laughter. In a little while "always thinking of Mary as much a part of himself as 'the beating of my heart,' he began to see the spirit of Mary shining out in Georgina, and to find old times coming back 'so that the past can hardly be separated from the present.' " *

Dickens had been poor too long not to like to live in style when he was able to, with the consequence that about this time he found himself very uncomfortably in debt. He decided to let his house and go to Italy to economize. He spent a year there, chiefly at Genoa, and did a good deal of sightseeing in the peninsula; but he was too insular, too ill-read, for the experience to have any spiritual effect on him. He remained the typical British tourist. On the other hand he formed a friendship with a Mrs. de la Rue, the wife of a Swiss banker,

* Una Pope-Hennessy. *Charles Dickens.*

who was living at Genoa. She suffered, it appeared, from delusions, and Dickens, who had taken an interest in hypnotism, was convinced that by means of this he could rid her of them. The pair met every day, sometimes twice a day, so that he could pursue the treatment. It made Kate very uneasy. On their excursions the de la Rues went everywhere with the Dickenses, and such was the efficacy of Charles' ministrations that Mrs. de la Rue was restored to health; but Kate was relieved when they went back to England.

She was placid and of a melancholic disposition. She was not adaptable and liked neither the journeys Charles took her on, the parties she went to with him, nor the parties in which she acted as hostess. She was colorless, and rather stupid it would appear, and it is likely enough that the great and important people who were eager to enjoy the celebrated author's company found it a nuisance to have to put up with his dull wife. Some of them to her annoyance persistently treated her as a cipher. It is not easy to be the wife of a distinguished man. She is unlikely to make a good job of it unless she has tact or a lively sense of humor. In default of these, and there is no sign that Kate had either, she must love her husband. Kate does not appear ever to have been in love with Dickens. There is a letter he wrote to her during their engagement in which he reproaches her for her coldness. It may be that she married him because at that time marriage was the only occupation open to a woman, or it may be that, as the eldest of eight daughters, some pressure was put upon her by her parents to embrace an offer that provided for her future. She was a kindly, gracious, gentle little thing, but incapable of meeting the claims which her husband's eminence made upon her.

Meanwhile Georgy was there to take the place that Mary once occupied. In course of time Dickens came to depend more and more on her. They took long walks together and he discussed his literary plans with her. She acted as his amanuensis. Having once learned how pleasant (and economical) it was to live abroad Dickens began to spend long periods on the Continent. Georgy, as one of the family, went with them to Italy and later on to Lausanne, Boulogne and Paris. On one occasion, when they were going to settle in Paris for a considerable time, she went there alone with Charles to find an apartment

while Kate waited in England till they had made everything ready for her. During Kate's pregnancies Georgy
accompanied Dickens on the jaunts he was fond of taking, went to parties with him and often presided at his
table in Kate's place. One would have expected Kate to
resent the situation; she does not seem to have done so.

The years passed. In 1857 Charles Dickens was forty-
five. He was the most popular author in England, with
a reputation besides as a social reformer, and he lived,
as very much appealed to his theatrical instincts, in the
public eye. His children were grown up. An unforeseen
event occurred. He was always fond of acting and had
on more than one occasion given amateur performances
of one play or another for charitable purposes. He was
asked at this time to give some performances in Manchester of a play, *The Frozen Deep,* which Wilkie Collins
had written with his help, and which had been performed with great success before the Queen, the Prince
Consort and the King of the Belgians. Dickens grew a
beard to play the part of a self-sacrificing arctic explorer,
a part which he vastly enjoyed and played with such
pathos that there was not a dry eye in the house. But
when he agreed to repeat the play at Manchester, since
he did not think his daughters, who had taken the girls'
parts before, would be heard in a big theater he decided
that their parts should be acted by professionals. A
young woman called Ellen Ternan was engaged for one
of them. He had seen her some months before in a play
called *Atalanta,* and going to her dressing room, found
her in tears because she had to show so much leg. He
was charmed with her modesty.

Ellen Ternan was eighteen. She was small, fair and
blue-eyed. The rehearsals took place in Dickens' house
and he directed. He was flattered by Ellen's adoring attitude and by her pathetic anxiety to please him. Before
the rehearsals were over he was desperately in love with
her. He gave her a bracelet, which by mistake was delivered to his wife, and she naturally made him a scene;
but Charles seems to have adopted the attitude of injured innocence which a husband in such an awkward
junction finds it most convenient to adopt. The play was
produced and his performance electrified the audience.

Kate had not given him all he had expected of her and
now, infatuated with Ellen Ternan, he grew more and

more intolerant of his wife's shortcomings: "she is amiable and complying," he wrote, "but nothing on earth would make her understand me." He began to think she had never suited him. He told John Forster that "the gist is that it is a mistake to marry too young and that the years are not making things easier." He had developed, but she had remained what she was at the beginning. Dickens was quite convinced that he had nothing to reproach himself with. There is something of Pecksniff in the way he assured himself that he had been a good father and had done everything possible for his children. Though he was none too pleased at having to provide for so many, for which he seems to have thought Kate alone was to blame, he liked them well enough when they were small; but as they grew up he lost interest in them and at a suitable age packed most of the boys off to remote parts of the world.

During this time he was moody, restless and out of temper with everyone but Georgy. At last he came to the conclusion that he could not live with Kate any longer, but his position with the public was such that he was fearful of the scandal that an open break might cause. His anxiety is comprehensible. He had been for years the moving advocate of hearth and home, and had done more than anyone to make Christmas the symbolic festival to celebrate the domestic virtues and the beauty of a united and happy family life. Various suggestions were made. One was that Kate should have her own suite of rooms apart from his and act as hostess at his parties and accompany him to public functions. Another was that she should stay in London while he was at Gad's Hill (a house in Kent he had recently bought) and stay at Gad's Hill when he was in London. A third was that she should settle abroad. All these proposals she rejected, and finally a complete separation was decided on. Kate was installed in a little house on the edge of Camden Town with an income of six hundred pounds a year. A little later Dickens' eldest son, Charley, was sent to live with her.

The arrangement is surprising. One cannot but wonder why Kate allowed herself to be driven from her own house and why she consented to leave her children behind. She knew of Charles' infatuation with Ellen Ternan and one would have supposed that, with this trump in her hand, she could have made what terms she chose. Placid as she was, and stupid as she may have been, the only explanation of Kate's submissiveness is that suggested by Dickens' mysterious allusion to a mental disorder "which caused his wife to think that she would be better away." This has been thought, though I do not know on what grounds, to be a discreet reference to the fact that Kate drank. If she had become a confirmed alcoholic it would explain why Georgy should have managed the house and looked after the children, why they should have remained at home when their mother left it, why Georgy could write that: "Poor Kate's incapacity for looking after children was no secret to anyone." It may be that Charley was sent to live with her to restrain her intemperance.

Dickens was too celebrated for his private affairs not to give rise to gossip. Many of his friends thought he had behaved badly and so excited his bitter hostility. Scandalous rumors were spread abroad not, as one would have supposed, about Ellen Ternan, but about Georgy. Dickens was furious and believing them to have emanated from the Hogarths, Kate's family and Georgy's, forced them by threatening to turn Kate out of her house without a penny to sign a declaration that they did not believe there was anything reprehensible in his relations with his sister-in-law. The Hogarths took a fortnight before they could bring themselves to be thus blackmailed. They must have known that if he carried out his threat Kate could go to law with a cast-iron case; if they dared not let things go to such lengths it can surely have been only because there were faults on Kate's side they were unwilling to have divulged.

Georgy is the enigmatic figure in the affair. The gossip attained such proportions that Dickens felt himself called upon to give the public his own version of the separation. In a letter published in the *New York Tribune* and later in English papers he wrote of Georgy: "Upon my soul and honour there is not on earth a more virtuous and spotless creature." By this, of course, he meant to deny that he had had sexual relations with her. It is very probably true. Perhaps Georgy loved him; she was jealous enough of Kate to cut out all sentences in praise of her when, after Charles' death, she edited a selection of his letters; but the attitude church and state had adopted towards marriage with a deceased wife's sister had given any connection of the sort an incestuous aspect, and it may never even have entered Georgy's head that there could be more between herself and the man in whose house she had lived for fifteen years than the fond affection a sister might legitimately feel for her brother by blood. Moreover, Charles was passionately enamored of Ellen Ternan. Perhaps it was enough for Georgy to be in the confidence of so celebrated a man and to have established a complete ascendancy over him. The strangest thing about the whole affair is that she welcomed Ellen Ternan to Gad's Hill—and made a friend of her.

Under the name of Charles Tringham, Dickens took a house for Ellen at Peckham, and not so long ago visitors, going to see it, were shown the tree under which Mr. Tringham, an author, had liked to sit. Here she lived till his death and here she bore him a son. It was not difficult to get from Gad's Hill to Peckham, and Dickens would spend two, and sometimes three, nights with Ellen. On one occasion they went to Paris together.

At about the time of the separation Dickens began to give readings of his work and for this purpose traveled all over the British Isles and again went to America. His histrionic gift served him well and his success was spectacular. But the effort he exerted and the constant journeys entailed wore him out, and people began to notice that though still in his forties he looked like an old man. But these readings were not his only activity: during the twelve years between his separation and his death he wrote three long novels and conducted an immensely successful magazine called *All the Year Round*. It is not surprising that his health failed. He was warned by his doctors that he must take care of himself, but, enraptured as he was by the applause he received from the public, he insisted on making a final tour. He was taken so ill in the middle of it that he had to abandon it. He went back to Gad's Hill and sat down to write *The Mystery of Edwin Drood*. But to make up to his managers for the readings he had had to cut short, he arranged to give twelve more in London. This was in January 1870. "The audiences at St. James's Hall were immense and sometimes they rose and cheered in a body as he entered as well as when he left."* Back at Gad's Hill he resumed work on *Edwin Drood*. One day in June, Georgy, with whom he was living alone, noticed at dinner that he looked very ill. "Come and lie down," she said. "Yes, on the ground," he answered. They were the last words he spoke. He slid from her arm and fell upon the floor. Georgy sent for his two daughters, who were in London, and next day one of them, Katey, was despatched by the resourceful and competent woman to break the news to his wife. Katey returned to Gad's Hill with Ellen Ternan. He died next day, June 9th, 1870, and was buried in Westminster Abbey.

In this sketch of Dickens' life I have said nothing of his persistent and efficacious interest in social reform and of his passionate championship of the poor and oppressed. I have confined myself, as far as I could, to his private life, since it seemed to me that to know something of this must give a greater interest to the book I am inviting the reader to read. *David Copperfield* is in great part autobiographical; but Dickens was writing a novel, not an autobiography, and though he drew much of his material from his own life he made such use of it as suited his purpose. For the rest he fell back on his fertile imagination. Mr. Micawber and Dora, as I have already remarked, were drawn after his father and his first love, Maria Beadnell; Agnes partly from his idealized memories of Mary Hogarth and partly after her sister Georgy. David Copperfield at the age of ten was put to work by his wicked stepfather, as Charles Dickens was by *his* father, and suffered in the same way from the "degradation" of having to mix with boys of his own age whom he did not consider his social equals.

David Copperfield tells his story himself. This is a device that novelists have often used. It has its advantages and disadvantages. One advantage is that it forces the author to keep to the thread of his narrative; he can only tell you what he has himself seen, heard or done. It served Dickens well since his plots were apt to be complicated and confused, and the reader's interests was sometimes diverted to characters and incidents that had no bearing on the course of the story. In *David Copperfield* there is only one major digression, and that is the account of Dr.

* Una Pope-Hennessy. *Charles Dickens.*

Strong's relations with his wife, her mother and his wife's cousin: it does not concern David and is in itself tedious. The device has the other advantage of lending verisimilitude to the story and enlisting your sympathy with the narrator. You may approve of him or disapprove of him, but he concentrates your attention on himself and so compels your sympathy.

A disadvantage of the device is that the narrator, who is also the hero, cannot without immodesty tell you that he is handsome and attractive; he is apt to seem vainglorious when he relates his doughty deeds and stupid when he fails to see what is obvious to the reader, that the heroine loves him. A greater disadvantage, and one that no authors of this sort of novel have been able entirely to surmount, is that the hero-narrator, the central character, is likely to appear pallid in comparison with the persons he comes in contact with. I have asked myself why this should be, and the only explanation I can suggest is that the author, since the hero is himself, sees him from the inside, subjectively, and telling what he sees, gives him the confusions, the weaknesses, the indecisions he feels in himself; whereas he sees the other characters from the outside, objectively, through his imagination; and if he is an author with Dickens' peculiar gifts, he sees them with a dramatic intensity, with an unfailing sense of fun, with a keen eye for their oddity, and so makes them stand out with a vividness that overshadows his portrait of himself.

Dickens did all he could to excite the reader's sympathy for his hero, and indeed on the celebrated journey to Dover when he ran away to seek the protection of his aunt Betsey Trotwood, an admirable character, he loads his dice somewhat extravagantly. One cannot be but surprised that the little boy should have been such a ninny as to let everyone he came across rob and cheat him. After all, he had been in the factory for some months and had wandered about London early and late, he had lived with the Micawbers and pawned their bits and pieces for them, and had visited them at the Marshalsea; one would have thought that if he were the bright boy he is described to be, even at that tender age he would have acquired some knowledge of the world and enough sharpness to fend for himself. But throughout David Copperfield shows himself sadly incompetent.

He continues to allow himself to be robbed and cheated. He never seems able to cope with a difficulty. His weakness with Dora, his lack of common sense in dealing with the ordinary problems of domestic life, are really almost more than one can bear; and he is so obtuse that he does not guess that Agnes is in love with him. I cannot persuade myself that in the end he became the successful novelist we are told he did. If he wrote novels, I suspect they were more like the novels of Mrs. Henry Wood than the novels of Charles Dickens. It is strange that his creator should have given him none of his own drive, vitality and exuberance. David was slim and good looking; and he had charm, or he would not have attracted the affection of almost everyone he encountered; he was honest, kindly and conscientious; but he was surely a bit of a fool. He remains the least interesting person in the book.

But that doesn't matter: it is filled with characters of the most astonishing variety, vividness and originality. They are not realistic and yet they abound with life. There never were such people as the Micawbers, Peggotty and Barkis, Traddles, Betsey Trotwood and Mr. Dick, Uriah Heep and his mother. They are fantastic inventions of Dickens' exultant imagination, but they have so much vigor, they are so consistent, they are presented with so much verisimilitude and with so much conviction, that you believe in them. They are extravagant, but not unreal, and when you have once come to know them you can never quite forget them. The most remarkable of them is, of course, Mr. Micawber. He never fails you. Dickens has been blamed, to my mind unjustly, for making him end up as a respectable magistrate in Australia, and some critics have thought that he should have remained reckless and improvident to the last page. Australia was a sparsely settled country; Mr. Micawber was a man of fine presence, of some education and of grandiloquent address. I do not see why in that environment and with those advantages he should not have attained an official position. I am less willing to believe that he would have been ingenious enough and secret enough to discover the villainy of Uriah Heep.

Dickens never hesitated to make use of coincidence when it suited his story, and was not bothered by the necessity the modern novelist is under to make events not only likely, but so far as possible, inevitable. Readers then accepted the grossest improbabilities without turning a hair, and such was Dickens' intensity, so great his narrative skill, one is prepared to accept them to this day. *David Copperfield* abounds in coincidences. When Steerforth returns to England and his ship is wrecked on the sands of Yarmouth, who should have gone there just then to see some friends but David? Dickens was quite skilful enough to have avoided this shocking improbability if he had wanted to. He didn't, because it gave him the opportunity for a striking scene.

Though *David Copperfield* has fewer of the melodramatic incidents than Dickens was in the habit of using in his novels, it must be admitted that certain of the characters smack of what used to be called transpontine melodrama. Uriah Heep, for instance; but for all that he is a powerful, horrifying figure admirably portrayed; a lesser creation, Steerforth's servant, has a mysterious, sinister quality which sends cold shivers down one's back. The most baffling character of this type is to my mind Rosa Dartle. She has generally been looked upon as a failure. I have a notion that Dickens meant to make greater use of her in his story than he did, and I suspect (without any evidence) that if he did not do so it was because he feared to offend his public. I have asked myself whether Steerforth had not been her lover and whether her hatred of him was not mingled with a hungry, jealous love. I cannot see what else could have caused her to treat Littly Em'ly (a stagey figure who, to my mind, got what she asked for) with such callousness.

Dickens wrote: "Of all my books I like this one best; like many fond parents I have my favourite child and his name is David Copperfield." An author is not always a good judge of his own work, but in this case Dickens' judgment was sound. Matthew Arnold and Ruskin considered it his best novel and I think we may agree with them. If we do, we shall be in pretty good company.

FYODOR DOSTOEVSKY

and

THE BROTHERS KARAMAZOV

FYODOR DOSTOEVSKY was born in 1821. His father, a surgeon at the Hospital of St. Mary in Moscow, was a member of the nobility, a fact to which the novelist seems to have attached importance, since he was distressed when on his condemnation his rank, such as it was, was taken away from him, and on his release from prison he pressed influential friends to have it restored to him. But nobility in Russia was different from what it is in other European countries; it could be acquired, for instance, by reaching a certain modest rank in the government service and appears to have had little more significance than to set you apart from the peasant and the tradesman and to allow you to look upon yourself as a gentleman. In point of fact Dostoevsky's family belonged to the white-collar class of poor professional men. His father was a stern man. He deprived himself not only of luxury, but even of comfort in order to give his seven children a good education; and from their earliest years he taught them that they must accustom themselves to hardship and misfortune to prepare themselves for the duties and obligations of life. They lived crowded together in the two or three rooms at the hospital which were the doctor's quarters. They were never allowed to go out alone, they were given no pocket money, they had no friends. The doctor had some private practice besides his hospital salary, and in course of time acquired a small property some hundred miles from Moscow and here, from then on, mother and children spent the summer. It was their first taste of freedom.

When Dostoevsky was sixteen his mother died, and his father took his two elder sons, Michael and Fyodor, to St. Petersburg to put them to school at the Military Engineering Academy. Michael, the elder, was rejected on account of his poor physique, and Fyodor was thus parted from the only person he cared for. He was lonely and unhappy. His father either would not or could not send him money, and he was unable to buy such necessities of life as books and boots, or even pay the regular charges of the institution. The doctor, having settled his elder sons and parked three other children with an aunt in Moscow, gave up his practice and retired with his two youngest daughters to his property in the country. He took to drink. He had been severe with his children; he was brutal with his serfs, and one day they murdered him.

This was in 1839. Fyodor worked well, though without enthusiasm, and having completed his term at the Academy was appointed to the Engineering Department of the Ministry of War. What with his share of his father's estate and his salary, he had now five thousand rubles a year. He rented an apartment, conceived an expensive passion for billiards, flung money away right and left, and when a year later he resigned his commission because he found service in the Engineering Department "as dull as potatoes" he was deeply in debt. He remained in debt till the last years of his life. He was an incorrigible spendthrift. His thriftlessness drove him to despair, but he never acquired the self-control to resist his caprices. It has been suggested by one of his biographers that his want of self-confidence was to an extent responsible for his habit of squandering money, since it gave him a passing sense of power and so gratified his vanity. It will be seen later to what mortifying straits his unhappy failing reduced him.

While still at the Academy Dostoevsky had begun a novel and now, having decided to earn his living as a writer, he finished it. It was called *Poor Folk*. He knew no one in the literary world, but an acquaintance, Grigorovich by name, knew a man, Nekrasov, who was proposing to start a review, and offered to show him the story. One day Dostoevsky came home late. He had spent the evening reading his novel to a friend and discussing it with him. At four in the morning he walked home. He felt he could not go to bed, and sat at the open window, looking at the night. He was startled by a ring. "It was Grigorovich and Nekrasov! Rushing into the room in transports and almost in tears they embraced me again and again." They had begun to read the book, taking it in turns to read aloud, and when they had finished decided, late though it was, to seek Dostoevsky out. "Never mind if he is asleep," they said to one another, "let us wake him. This thing transcends sleep." Nekrasov took the manuscript next day to Belinsky, the most important critic of the time, and he was as enthusiastic as had been the other two. The novel was published, and Dostoevsky found himself famous.

He did not take success well. A certain Madame Panaev-Golovachev has described the impression he made when he was brought to her apartment. "At the first glance one could perceive that the newcomer was a young man of an extremely nervous and impressionable temperament. Short and thin, he had fair hair, an unhealthy complexion, small grey eyes which wandered uneasily from object to object and pale lips which maintained a restless twitching. Almost everyone present was known to him, yet he seemed bashful, and took no part in the general conversation, even though successive members of the company tried to draw him out, to banish his reserve, and to make him feel that he was a member of our circle. After that evening, however, he came frequently to see us, and his restraint began to wear off: he even took to . . . engaging in disputes in which sheer contradictoriness seemed to impel him to give everyone the lie. The truth was that his youthfulness combined with his nervous temperament to deprive him of all self-control, and to lead him to over-parade his presumption and conceit as a writer. That is to say, dazed with his sudden and brilliant entry into the literary arena, and overwhelmed with the praises of the great ones in the world of letters, he, like most over-impressionable spirits, could not conceal his triumph over young litterateurs whose entry had been of a more modest order. . . . Through his captiousness and his tone of overweening pride, he showed that he considered himself to be immeasurably superior to his companions. . . . Particularly did Dostoevsky suspect all and sundry of attempting to pooh-pooh his talent; and since he discerned in every guileless word a desire to belittle his work, and to affront him personally, it was in a mood of seething resentment which yearned to pick a quarrel, to vent upon his fancied detractors the whole measure of spleen that was choking his breast, that he used to visit our house." *

Not an easy guest and not an engaging character. On the strength of his success he signed contracts to write a novel and a number of stories. With the advances he received he proceeded to lead so dissipated a life that his friends remonstrated with him. He quarreled with them, even with Belinsky, who had done so much for him, because he was not convinced of "the purity of his admiration," for he had persuaded himself that he was a genius and the greatest of Russian writers. His debts increased and he was obliged to work with haste. He had long suffered from an obscure nervous disorder, and now, falling ill, feared he was going mad or falling into a consumption. The stories written in these circumstances were failures, and the novel proved unreadable. The people who had so extravagantly praised him now attacked him, and the opinion was general that he was written out.

But his literary career was suddenly brought to an end. He had joined a group of young men, imbued with the socialistic notions then current in Western Europe, who were bent upon certain measures of reform, especially with the emancipation of the serfs and the abolition of censorship; they were harmless enough and seem to have done little more than meet once a week to discuss their ideas; but the police had the group under surveillance, and one day they were arrested and taken to the Fortress of Peter-Paul. They were tried and condemned to be shot. One winter morning they were taken to the place of execution, but as the soldiers prepared to carry out the sentence, a messenger arrived to say that the penalty was commuted to penal servitude in Siberia. Dostoevsky was sentenced to four years' imprisonment at Omsk, after which he was to serve as a common soldier. When he was taken back to the Fortress of Peter-Paul he wrote the following letter to his brother Michael:

"Today the 22nd of December, we were all taken to Semenovsky Square. There the death sentence was read to us, we were given the Cross to kiss, the dagger was broken over our heads, and our funeral toilet (white shirts) was made. Then three of us were put standing

---

* Quoted by Soloviev: *Dostoievsky, His Life and Literary Activity;* translated by C. J. Hogarth.

before the palisades for the execution of the death sentence. I was sixth in the row; we were called up by groups of three, and so I was in the second group, and had not more than a moment to live. I thought of you, my brother, and of yours; in that last moment you alone were in my mind; then first I learnt how very much I love you, my beloved brother! I had time to embrace Plestcheiv and Dourov, who stood near me, and to take my leave of them. Finally, retreat was sounded, those who were bound to the palisades were brought back, and it was read to us that His Imperial Majesty granted us our lives. Then the final sentences were recited. Palm alone is fully pardoned. He has been transferred to the line with the same rank."

In one of his best books Dostoevsky has described the horrors of his life in prison. One point is worthy of remark. He notes that within two hours of arriving a newcomer would find himself at home with the other convicts and live on familiar terms with them. "But with a gentleman, a nobleman, things were different. No matter how unassuming and good-tempered and intelligent he might be, he would to the end remain a person unanimously hated and despised, and never understood and still more, never trusted. No one would ever come to look upon him as a friend or a comrade, and though, as the years went on, he might at least attain the point of ceasing to serve as a butt for insult, he would still be powerless to live his own life, or to get rid of the torturing thought that he was lonely and a stranger."

Now Dostoevsky was not such a great gentleman as all that; his origins were as humble as his life, but for his brief period of glory, had been poverty-stricken. Dourov, his friend and fellow-prisoner, was loved by all. It looks very much as though Dostoevsky's loneliness and the suffering it caused him were in part at least occasioned by his own defects of character, his conceit, his egoism, his suspiciousness and his quarrelsomeness. But his loneliness, amid hundreds of companions, drove him back on himself: "Through this spiritual isolation," he writes, "I gained an opportunity of reviewing my past life, of dissecting it down to the pettiest detail, of probing my heretofore existence, and of judging myself strictly and inexorably." The New Testament was the only book he was allowed to possess, and he read it incessantly. Its influence on him was profound. From then on he preached and (as far as his wilful nature permitted) practiced humility and the necessity of suppressing the human desires of normal men. "Before all things humble yourself," he wrote, "consider what your past life has been, consider what you may be able to effect in the future, consider how great a mass of meanness and pettiness and turpitude lies lurking at the bottom of your soul." Prison cowed his overweening, imperious spirit. He left it a revolutionary no longer, but a firm upholder of the authority of the crown and the established order. He left it also an epileptic.

When his term of imprisonment came to an end he was sent to complete his sentence as a private in a small garrison town in Siberia. It was a hard life, but he accepted its pains as part of the punishment he merited for his crime, for he had come to the conclusion that his mild activities for reform were sinful; and he wrote to his brother: "I do not complain; this is my cross and I have deserved it." In 1856 through the intercession of an old schoolfellow he was raised from the ranks and his life became more tolerable. He made friends, and he fell in love. The object of his affections was a certain Maria Dmitrievna Isaeva, wife of a political deportee who was dying of drink and consumption, and mother of a young son; she is described as a rather pretty blonde of middle height, very thin, passionate and *exaltée*. Little seems to be known of her, except that she was of a nature as suspicious, as jealous and as self-tormenting as was Dostoevsky himself. He became her lover. But after some time Isaev, her husband, was moved from the village in which Dostoevsky was stationed to another frontier post some four hundred miles away and there died. Dostoevsky wrote and proposed marriage. The widow hesitated, partly because they were both destitute and partly because she had lost her heart to a "high-minded and sympathetic" young teacher called Vergunov and had become his mistress. Dostoevsky, deeply in love, was frantic with jealousy, but with his passion for lacerating himself and perhaps with his novelist's passion for seeing himself as a character of fiction, he did a characteristic thing. Declaring Vergunov to be dearer to him than a brother, he besought one of his friends to send him money so as to make it possible for Maria Isaeva to marry her lover.

He was able, however, to play the part of a man with a breaking heart sacrificing himself to the happiness of his well-beloved without serious consequences, for the widow had an eye to the main chance. Vergunov, though "high-minded and sympathetic," was penniless, whereas Dostoevsky was now an officer, his pardon could not be long delayed, and there was no reason why he should not again write successful books. The couple were married in 1857. They had no money, and Dostoevsky had borrowed till he could borrow no more. He turned again to literature; but as an ex-convict he had to get permission to publish, and this was not easy. Nor was married life. In fact it was very unsatisfactory, which Dostoevsky ascribed to his wife's suspicious, painfully fanciful nature. It escaped his notice that he was himself as impatient, irritable, neurotic and unsure of himself as he had been in the first flush of success. He began various pieces of fiction, put them aside, began others and in the end produced little and that little of no importance.

In 1859, as the result of his appeals and by the influence of friends, he succeeded in getting back to St. Petersburg. Ernest Simmons in his book on Dostoevsky justly remarks that the means he employed to regain his freedom were abject. "He wrote patriotic poems, one celebrating the birthday of the Dowager Empress Alexandra, another on the coronation of Alexander II, and a threnody on the death of Nicholas I. Begging letters were addressed to people in power and to the new Tsar himself. In them he protests that he adores the young monarch whom he describes as a sun shining on the just and the unjust alike, and he declares that he is ready to give up his life for him. The crime for which he was convicted he readily confesses to, but insists that he has repented and is now suffering for opinions that he had abandoned."

He settled down in the capital with his wife and stepson, and together with his brother Michael started a literary journal. It was called *Time* and for it he wrote *The House of the Dead* and *The Insulted and Injured*. It was a success, and for the next two years his circumstances were easy. In 1862, leaving the magazine in charge of Michael, he visited Western Europe. He was not pleased with it. He found Paris "a most boring town," and its people money-grubbing and small-minded. He was shocked by the misery of the London poor and the hypocritical respectability of the well-to-do. He went to Italy, but he was not interested in art, and he spent a week in Florence reading the four volumes of Victor Hugo's *Les Misérables*. He returned to Russia without seeing Rome or Venice. His wife had contracted tuberculosis and was now a chronic invalid.

Some months before he went abroad Dostoevsky, being then forty, had made the acquaintance of a young woman who brought a short story for publication in his journal. Her name was Polina Suslova. She was twenty, a virgin and handsome, but to show that her views were advanced she bobbed her hair and wore dark glasses. After Dostoevsky's return to St. Petersburg they became lovers. Then, owing to an unfortunate article by one of his contributors, the magazine was suppressed and he decided to go abroad again. The reason he gave was to get treatment for his epilepsy, which had for some time been growing worse, but this was only an excuse; he wanted to go to Wiesbaden to gamble, for he had invented a system to break the bank, and he had made a date with Polina Suslova in Paris. He borrowed money from the Fund for Needy Authors and set out.

At Wiesbaden he lost much of his money and tore himself from the tables only because his passion for Polina Suslova was stronger than his passion for gambling. They had arranged to go to Rome together, but while waiting for him the emancipated young lady had had a short affair with a Spanish medical student; she was upset when he walked out on her, a proceeding women are not apt to take with equanimity, and refused to resume her relations with Dostoevsky. He accepted the situation and proposed that they should go to Italy "as brother and sister," and to this, being presumably at a loose end, she consented. The arrangement, complicated by the fact that they were so short of money they had on occasion to pawn their knickknacks, was not a success, and after some weeks of "lacerations" they parted. Dostoevsky went back to Russia. He found his wife dying. Six months later she died. He wrote as follows to a friend:

My wife, the being who adored me, and whom I loved beyond measure, expired at Moscow, whither she had removed a year before her death of consumption. I followed her thither and never once throughout that winter left her bedside. . . . My friend, she loved me beyond measure, and I returned her affection to a degree transcending all expression; yet our joint life was not a happy one. Some day, when I meet you, I will tell you the whole story. But for the present let me confine myself to saying that, apart from the fact that we lived unhappily together, we should never have lost our mutual love for one another, but have become more attached in proportion to our misery. This may seem to you strange; yet it is but the truth. She was the best, the noblest, woman that I have ever known. . . .

Dostoevsky somewhat exaggereated his devotion. During that winter he went twice to St. Petersburg in connection with a new magazine he had started with his brother. It was no longer liberal in tendency, as *Time* had been, and it failed. Michael died after a short illness, leaving twenty-five thousand rubles of debts, and Dostoevsky found himself obliged to support Michael's widow and children, his mistress and her child. He borrowed ten thousand rubles from a rich aunt, but by 1865 had to declare himself bankrupt. He owed sixteen thousand rubles on note of hand and five thousand on the security of his word alone. His creditors were troublesome, and to escape from them he again borrowed money from the Fund for Needy Authors and got an advance on a novel which he contracted to deliver by a certain date. Thus provided, he went to Wiesbaden to try his luck once more at the tables and to meet Polina Suslova. He offered her marriage, but such love as she had had for him was now turned to hatred. One may surmise that she had become his mistress because he was a well-known author and as the editor of a magazine might be of use to her. But the magazine was dead. His appearance had always been insignificant, and now he was forty-five, bald and epileptic. It is understandable that his sexual pretensions exasperated her beyond endurance; for nothing makes a woman more impatient than the desire of a man to whom she is not physically attracted; and she left him to go back to Paris. He lost all his money at the tables and was obliged to pawn his watch. He had to sit quietly in his room so as not to get up an appetite which he had not the means to satisfy. He began another book, under the lash, he says, and of necessity and against time. He was penniless, ill and wretched. The book he was writing under these conditions was *Crime and Punishment*.

Desperately in need of cash, he applied to everyone he knew, even to Turgenev, with whom he had quarreled and whom he both hated and despised; but he took his money and with it returned to Russia. But while still at work on *Crime and Punishment* he remembered that he had contracted to deliver a book by a certain date. By the iniquitous agreement he had signed, if he did not do so the publisher had the right to issue everything he wrote for the following nine years without paying him a penny. Some bright person suggested that he should employ a stenographer; this he did and in twenty-six days finished a novel called *The Gambler*. The stenographer was twenty, but homely; she was, however, efficient, practical, patient, devoted and admiring; and early in the year 1867 he married her. His relations, fearing that he would not thenceforward help them as much as before, were displeased, and treated his young wife so badly that she persuaded him to leave Russia once more. He was again heavily in debt.

This time he stayed away four years. At first Anna Grigorievna, for such was his wife's name, found life difficult with the celebrated author. His epilepsy grew worse. He was irritable, thoughtless and vain. He renewed his correspondence with Polina Suslova, which did not conduce to poor Anna's peace of mind, but being a young woman of uncommon good sense she kept her dissatisfaction to herself. They went to Baden-Baden, and there he again began to gamble. He again lost all he had and as usual wrote to everyone likely to help for money and more money, and whenever it arrived slunk off to the tables to lose it. They pawned whatever they had of value, they moved into cheaper and cheaper lodgings, and sometimes had hardly enough to eat. Anna Grigorievna was pregnant. Here is a bit of one of his letters: he had just won four thousand francs.

"Anna Grigorievna begged me to be content with the four thousand francs, and to leave at once. But there was a chance, so easy and possible to remedy everything. And the examples? Besides one's own personal winnings, one sees every day others winning 20,000 and 30,000 francs (one does not see those who lose). Are there saints in the world? Money is more necessary to me than to them. I staked more than I lost. I began to lose my last resources, enraging myself to fever point. I lost. I pawned my clothes, Anna Grigorievna has pawned everything that she has, her last trinkets. (What an angel!) How she consoled me, how she wearied in that accursed Baden in our two little rooms above the forge where we had to take refuge! At last, no more, everything was lost. (Oh, those Germans are vile. They are all, without exception, usurers, scoundrels and rascals. The proprietor, knowing that we had nowhere to go till we received money, raised his prices.) At last we had to escape and leave Baden."

His first child was born at Geneva, and Dostoevsky was enchanted. But he continued to gamble. He was bitterly repentant because his weakness lost the money which would have provided his wife and child with the necessities they so badly needed. This, however, did not prevent him from returning to the gambling house whenever he had a few francs in his pocket. After three months, to his intense grief, the child died. Anna Grigorievna was again pregnant, but he felt he could never love another child as passionately as the little girl he had lost. *Crime and Punishment* had been a great success, and he was already at work on another book. It was called *The Idiot*. His publisher sent him two hundred rubles a month, but this did not prevent him from being in continual straits, and he was continually asking for further advances. *The Idiot* failed to please and he started on yet another short novel, *The Eternal Husband*, and then on a long one called in English *The Possessed*. Meanwhile, according to circumstances, which I take it to mean when they had exhausted their credit, Dostoevsky, his wife and child moved from place to place. But they were homesick. He had never overcome his dislike of Europe. He was untouched by the culture and distinction of Paris, the *gemütlichkeit*, the music of Germany, the splendor of the Alps, the deep, but smiling beauty of the lakes of Switzerland, the gracious loveliness of Tuscany and that treasury of art which is Florence. He found Western civilization bourgeois, decadent and corrupt, and convinced himself of its approaching dissolution. "I am becoming dull and narrow here," he wrote from Milan, "and am losing touch with Russia. I lack the Russian air and the Russian people." He felt he could never finish *The Possessed* unless he went back to Russia. Anna was pining to go home. But they had no money, and Dostoevsky's publisher had already advanced more than the book could be expected to earn. In desperation Dostoevsky appealed to him again. The first two numbers had already appeared in a magazine and, faced with the fear of getting no further instalments, he sent money for the fares. The Dostoevskys returned to St. Petersburg.

This was in 1871. Dostoevsky was fifty and had ten more years to live.

He had become a passionate Slavophil and looked to Russia to save the world. *The Possessed* was received with favor, and its attack on the young radicals of the day brought its author friends in reactionary circles. They thought he could be made use of in the government's struggle against reform and offered him the well-paid editorship of a paper called *The Citizen*, which was officially supported. He held it for a year and then resigned owning to a disagreement with his employer over a proposal which, reactionary though he now too was, proved more than he could swallow. But by this time the good and practical Anna had started a publishing business of her own and brought out editions of her husband's works so profitably that for the rest of his life he was released from want. His remaining years can be passed over very briefly. Under the title of *The Journal of an Author* he wrote a number of occasional essays. They were immensely successful, and he came to look upon himself as a teacher and a prophet. This is a rôle which few writers have been disinclined to play. He wrote a novel called *A Raw Youth* and finally *The Brothers Karamazov*. His fame had increased, and when he died, rather suddenly, in 1881, he was esteemed by many the greatest writer of his time. His funeral is said to have been the occasion for "one of the most remarkable demonstrations of public feeling ever witnessed in the Russian capital."

I have tried to relate the main facts of Dostoevsky's life without comment. The impression one receives is of a singularly unamiable character. Vanity is an occupational disease of artists, whether writers, painters, musicians or actors, but Dostoevsky's was outrageous. It seems never to have occurred to him that anyone could have enough of hearing him talk about himself and his works. With this was combined, necessarily maybe, that lack of self-confidence which is now called the inferiority complex. It was perhaps on this account that he was so openly contemptuous of his fellow writers. A man of principle would hardly have been reduced by the experience of prison to such a miserable submission; but though he accepted his sentence as the due punishment for his sin in resisting authority, this did not prevent him from doing all he could to get it remitted. It hardly seems logical. I have related before to what depths of self-abasement he descended in his appeals to persons of power and influence. He was utterly lacking in self-control, but it may be that this should be ascribed to the epilepsy from which he so severely suffered, in which case he cannot be held responsible for it. Neither prudence nor common decency served to restrain him when he was in the grip of passion. So when his wife was dying he abandoned her to follow Polina Suslova to Paris and only rejoined her when that emancipated young woman threw him over. But his weakness is nowhere more manifest than in his mania for gambling. It reduced him time after time to destitution. In Geneva he was obliged to borrow sums of five and ten francs to buy food for himself and his wife.

The reader will remember that to fulfil a contract he wrote a short novel called *The Gambler*. It is not a good one, but it is interesting in that the heroine, Polina Alexandrovna, was apparently suggested by Polina Suslova, and offers an early sketch of a type, the woman whose love is comingled with hatred, which he drew with greater elaboration in later books. It has the added interest that in it Dostoevsky very acutely describes the feelings he knew so well which seize the unfortunate victim of the gambler's passion; and after you have read it you understand how it came about that notwithstanding the humiliations it caused him, the misery to him and those he loved, the dishonorable proceedings it occasioned (when he got money from the Fund for Needy Authors it was to enable him to write, not to gamble), the constant need to apply to friends, already wearied of providing him with money, notwithstanding everything he could not resist the temptation. He was an exhibitionist, as to a greater or less extent are all those who, whatever art they practice, have the creative instinct; and he has described vividly the way in which a run of luck may gratify the discreditable tendency. The onlookers crowd round and stare at the fortunate gambler as though he were a superior being. They wonder and admire. He is the center of attention. Balm to the unhappy man cursed with a morbid diffidence! When he wins it gives him an intoxicating sense of power; he feels himself the master of his fate, for his cleverness, his intuition are so infallible that he can control chance.

"I have only for once to show will power and in one hour I can transform my destiny," he makes his gambler exclaim. "The great thing is will power. Only remember what happened to me seven months ago at Roulettenburg just before my final failure. Oh! it was a remarkable instance of determination: I had lost everything then, everything. . . . I was going out of the Casino, I looked, there was still one gulden in my waistcoat pocket: 'Then I shall have something for dinner,' I thought. But after I had gone a hundred paces I changed my mind and went back. I staked that gulden . . . and there really is something peculiar in the feeling when, alone in a strange land, far from home and from friends, not knowing whether you will have anything to eat that day—you stake your last gulden, your very last. I won, and twenty minutes later I went out of the Casino, having a hundred and seventy gulden in my pocket. That's a fact. That's what the last gulden can sometimes do. And what if I had lost heart then? What if I had not dared to risk it?"

Dostoevsky's life was written by a certain Strakhov, an old friend of his, and in connection with this work he wrote a letter to Tolstoy which Aylmer Maude has printed in his biography of that author and which, with some omissions, I now give in his translation:

"All the time I was writing I had to fight against a feeling of disgust and tried to suppress my bad feelings. . . . I cannot regard Dostoevsky as a good or happy man. He was bad, debauched, full of envy. All his life long he was a prey to passions that would have rendered him ridiculous and miserable had he been less intelligent or less wicked. I was vividly aware of these feelings while writing his biography. In Switzerland, in my presence, he treated his servant so badly that the man revolted and said to him: 'But I too am a man!' I remember how I was struck by those words which reflected the ideas current in free Switzerland about the rights of man and were addressed to one who was always preaching sentiments of humanity to the rest of mankind. Such scenes were of constant occurrence; he could not control his temper . . . the worst of it was that he prided himself on the fact that he never repented of his dirty actions. Dirty actions attracted him and he gloried in the fact. Viskovatov (a professor) told me how Dostoevsky had boasted of having outraged a little girl at the bathhouse, who had been brought to him by her governess. . . . With all this he was given to a sort of mawkish sentimentality and to high-flown humanitarian dreams, and it is these dreams, his literary message and the tendency of his writings, which endear him to us. In a word, all these novels endeavor to exculpate their author, they show that the most hideous villainies can exist side by side with the noblest sentiments . . ."

It is true that his sentimentality was mawkish and his humanitarianism bootless. He had small acquaintance with the "people" to whom, as opposed to the intelligentsia, he looked for the regeneration of Russia, and he had little sympathy with their hard and bitter lot. He violently attacked the radicals who sought to alleviate it. The remedy he offered to the frightful misery of the poor "was to idealize their sufferings and make out of it a way of life. Instead of practical reforms, he offered them religious and mystical consolation." *

The story of the violation of the little girl has given pain to Dostoevsky's admirers, and they have discredited it. Strakhov's account is obviously based on hearsay; but to confirm it is a report that, overcome by remorse, Dostoevsky told it to an old friend who advised him by way of penance to confess it to the man whom he hated most in the world, whereupon he related it to Turgenev. But for all that it may not be true. Of course it is a fact that the theme crops up in his works with persistence, and a suppressed chapter in *The Possessed* is said to have dealt with it. But that is no proof that he actually committed the ugly action. It may well have been a delusion connected with his epilepsy, a delusion so strong that it filled him with a sense of guilt; or it may be that, like

---

* Simmons: *Dostoevski.*

many another novelist, he made a character commit a crime for which he had an unfortunate inclination, but could not bring himself to commit.*

Dostoevsky was vain, suspicious, quarrelsome, cringing, selfish, boastful, unreliable, inconsiderate, narrow and intolerant. But that is not the whole story. While in prison he had learned that men may commit crimes of murder, lust or theft, and yet have qualities of courage, generosity and of loving kindness towards their fellows. He had learned that no man is all of a piece, but of a hotchpotch of nobility and baseness, of vice and virtue. Dostoevsky was the least censorious of men. He was charitable. He never refused money to a beggar or a friend. When himself destitute he managed to scrape up something to send to his sister-in-law and his brother's mistress, to his worthless stepson and to the drunken good-for-nothing, his younger brother Andrew. They sponged on him as he sponged on others, and far from resenting it he seems only to have been sorry that he could not do more for them than he did. He loved, admired and respected his wife Anna; he looked upon her as in every way superior to himself, and it is touching to learn that during the four years of his absence abroad he was tormented by the fear that, alone with him, she would grow bored. He had a loving heart, and he craved to be loved. He could hardly bring himself to believe that he had at last found someone who, notwithstanding his defects, of which he was only too conscious, loved him devotedly. Anna gave him the happiest years of his life.

Such was the man. But that was only the man. There is a dichotomy between the man and the writer, and I can think of no one in which it has been greater than it was in Dostoevsky. This dichotomy probably exists in all creative artists, but it is more conspicuous in authors than in others because their medium is words, and the contradiction between their behavior and their communication is more shocking. Compare the beautiful idealism of Shelley, his passion for freedom and his hatred of injustice, with his unfeeling selfishness and his callous indifference to the pain he caused. I have no doubt that many a composer, many a painter has been as selfish and

* Cf. Yarmolinsky: *Dostoevsky. A Life.*

as callous as Shelley, but the beauty of his music, the beauty of his pictures, ravishes our senses and we are not offended by the discrepancy between his production and his conduct. It may be that the creative gift, a normal faculty of childhood and early youth, if it persists after adolescence is a disease which can only flourish at the expense of normal human attributes and, just as the melon is sweetest when grown in pure manure, thrives best in a soil compounded of vicious traits.

There was in Dostoevsky more than the vain, irritable, weak egotist his biographers depict. There was the man who could create Alyosha, perhaps the most charming, sweet, gentle creature in all fiction. There was the man who could create the saintlike Father Zossima. Alyosha was designed to be the central figure of *The Brothers Karamazov* as is plainly enough shown by the first sentence of the book: "Alexey Fyodorovitch Karamazov was the third son of Fyodor Pavlovitch Karamazov, a land-owner well known in the district in his own day, and still remembered among us owing to his gloomy and tragic death, which happened thirteen years ago, and which I shall describe in its proper place." Dostoevsky was too practiced a novelist without intention to have begun his book with a definite statement that marks Alyosha out. But in the book as we have it he plays a subordinate rôle compared with that of his brothers Dmitri and Ivan. He passes in and out of the story and seems to have little influence on the persons who play their part in it. His own activity is concerned with a group of schoolboys whose doings, beyond showing Alyosha's charm and loving kindness, have nothing to do with the development of the theme.

The explanation is that *The Brothers Karamazov,* which runs in Mrs. Garnett's translation to 838 pages, is but a fragment of the novel Dostoevsky proposed to write. He intended in further volumes to continue the development of Alyosha, taking him through a number of vicissitudes, in which it is supposed he was to undergo the great experience of sin and finally through suffering achieve salvation. But death prevented Dostoevsky from carrying out his intention, and *The Brothers Karamazov* remains a fragment. It is nevertheless one of the greatest novels ever written and stands at the head of this small, wonderful group of works of fiction, apart from other novels, great as they may be, and of which two thrilling examples are *Wuthering Heights* and *Moby Dick*. It is a very rich book and I should only do it an injustice if I attempted to discuss it summarily. Dostoevsky had been pondering over it a long time, and he took more pains with it than his financial difficulties had allowed him to take with any novel since his first; he put into it all his agonizing doubts, his eagerness to believe what his reason rejected and his anxious quest for the meaning of life. I can only tell the reader what not to expect, for he has no right to demand of an author what he has neither the power nor the intention to give him. This is not a realistic book. Dostoevsky's gift of observation was small, and he did not seek verisimilitude. The behavior of the characters is not to be judged by the ordinary standards of common life. Their actions are wildly improbable and the motives of them madly inconsequential. They are not persons you recognize as you recognize the creatures of Jane Austen's or Flaubert's invention; they are personifications of passions, pride, lust, sensuality, hate. They are not copied from life and elaborated by the author's skill into persons more significant than life presents; but emanations of the author's tortured, warped, morbid sensibility. But though not lifelike, they palpitate with life.

The Brothers Karamazov suffers from the prolixity which Dostoevsky knew was a fault in many of his other books, but of which he could not cure himself. Even in a translation one can hardly fail to be conscious of the sloppiness of the writing. Dostoevsky was a great novelist, but a poor artist. His sense of humor was elementary and Madame Hohlakov, who provides the comic relief, is merely tiresome. The three younger women, Lise, Katerina Ivanovna and Grushenka, are poorly individualized; all three are hysterical, spiteful and malevolent. They want to dominate and torture the man they love and at the same time to submit themselves to him and suffer at his hands. Their conduct is unaccountable. In my brief account of Dostoevsky's life I have omitted to speak of two other women with whom he had relations more or less intimate, because, though they provided him with material that he made use of, their influence on his life was negligible. He was a sensualist and highly sexed, but I cannot persuade myself that he knew much about women. He seems to have divided them summarily into two classes: the meek self-sacrificing woman who is browbeaten, ill-treated and imposed upon; and the proud, domineering woman who is passionate, cruel and vindictive. It is likely that here he had in mind Polina Suslova, whom he loved because the suffering she caused him, the indignities she heaped upon him, were the fillip he needed to satisfy his masochism.

The men are drawn with a firmer hand. Old Karamazov, the besotted buffoon, is beautifully presented; his bastard son, Smerdyakov, is a masterpiece of the sinister; of Alyosha I have already briefly spoken. The old ruffian had two other sons: Dmitri is the sort of man whom the tolerant are apt to describe as his own worst enemy; he is a vulgar, drunken, boastful bully, recklessly extravagant and in no way particular how he gets the money to spend so foolishly; his idea of debauchery is pathetically schoolboyish, and the description of the binge he goes on with Grushenka is naive to the point of absurdity. His prattle about his honor is merely disgusting. He is in a way the central character of the book, and that to my mind is a defect, for he is so worthless a creature that you do not care what becomes of him. He is supposed to be attractive to women, as such men often are, but Dostoevsky has not shown what his attractiveness consists of. There is one point in his behavior that has always struck me as significant. He takes money, money that he has stolen, to give to Grushenka, with whom he was passionately in love, so that she may marry the man who first seduced her. It recalls the episode when Dostoevsky tried to borrow money so that Maria Isaeva, to whom he was engaged, should marry the "high-minded and sympathetic" teacher who was her lover. He gave Dmitri, as ruthless an egotist as he was himself, his own masochism. Is masochism in some strange way the ultimate assertion of the self?

So far I have carped and the reader may well ask why, if I make these objections, I claim that *The Brothers Karamazov* is one of the world's greatest novels. Well, in the first place it is of absorbing interest. Dostoevsky was not only a great novelist, but a very competent one, the two do not always go together, and he had a remarkable gift for the effective dramatization of a situation. It may be worth while to point out a method he was fond of in order to excite in the reader a tremulous susceptibility. He will bring the chief persons in his story together to discuss some action so outrageous that it is incomprehensible, and then will lead you to an understanding of it with all the skill of Gaboriau unraveling a mystery of crime. These long conversations have a thrilling interest, and he heightens the thrill by an ingenious device; his characters are agitated quite out of proportion to the words they utter; he describes them as trembling with emotion, green in the face or fearfully pallid, so that a significance the reader cannot account for is given to the most ordinary remarks; and presently he is so wrought up by these extravagant gestures that his own nerves are set on edge and he is prepared to receive a real shock when something happens which otherwise would have left him unmoved.

But this is merely a matter of technique; the greatness of *The Brothers Karamazov* depends on the greatness of its theme. Many critics have said this was the quest of God; I for my part should have said it was the problem of evil. And this brings me to Ivan, old Karamazov's second son, who is the most interesting, though perhaps the least sympathetic, character in the book. It may be, as has been suggested, that he is the mouthpiece of Dostoevsky's fundamental convictions. It is in the sections called *Pro and Contra* and *The Russian Monk,* which Dostoevsky considered the culminating points of his novel, that the theme is discussed. Of the two sections *Pro and Contra* is the more powerful. In it Ivan takes up the problem of evil, which to the human intelligence seems incompatible with the existence of a God who is all-powerful and all-good. As an example he gives the unmerited suffering of children. That men should suffer for their sins seems reasonable enough, but that innocent children should suffer revolts the heart as well as the head. Ivan is not interested in whether God created man or man God, he is willing to believe that God exists, but he cannot accept the cruelty of the world He created. Ivan insists that there is no reason for the innocent to suffer for the sins of the guilty; and if they do, and they do, God either is evil or does not exist. I will say no more: *Pro and Contra* is there for the reader to read. Dostoevsky never wrote with greater power. But when he had written it he was frightened of what he had done. The argument was cogent, but the conclusion repugnant to his own belief that the world for all its evil and suffering is beautiful because it is the creation of God. "If one loves all living things in the world, this love will justify suffering and all will share each other's guilt. Suffering for the sin of others will then become the moral duty of every true Christian." That is what Dostoevsky wanted to believe. And having written *Pro and Contra* he hastened to write a refutation. No one was better aware than he that he had not succeeded. The section is tedious and the refutation unconvincing.

The problem of evil still awaits solution, and Ivan Karamazov's indictment has not yet been answered.

HERMAN MELVILLE

and

MOBY DICK

I HAVE READ Raymond Weaver's *Herman Melville, Mariner and Mystic,* Lewis Mumford's *Herman Melville,* Charles Roberts Anderson's *Melville in the South Seas,* and William Ellery Sedgwick's *Herman Melville: The Tragedy of Mind.* I don't believe that I know much more about Herman Melville than I knew before.

According to Raymond Weaver an "uncircumspect critic at the time of Melville's centenary in 1919" wrote: "Owing to some odd psychological experience, that has never been definitely explained, his style of writing, his view of life underwent a complete change." I don't quite know why this unnamed critic should be described as uncircumspect. He hit upon the problem which must puzzle everyone who is interested in Melville. It is on this account that one scrutinizes every known detail of his life and reads his letters and books, books some of which can only be read by a determined effort of will, to discover some hint that may help to elucidate the mystery.

But first let us take the facts so far as they are made known to us by the biographers. On the face of it, but only on the face of it, they are simple enough.

Herman Melville was born in 1819. His father Allan Melville and his mother Maria Gansevoort were gentlefolk. Allan was a cultivated, traveled man and Maria an elegant, well-bred and pious woman. For the first five years of their marriage they lived at Albany and after that settled in New York, where Allan's business—he was an importer of French dry goods—for a time prospered, and where Herman was born. He was the third of their eight children. But by 1830 Allan Melville had fallen on evil days and moved back to Albany, where two years later he died bankrupt and, it is said, insane. He left his family penniless. Herman went to the Albany Classical

178

Institute for boys, and on leaving school in 1834 was employed as a clerk in the New York State Bank; in 1835 he worked in his brother Gansevoort's fur store and the following year on his uncle's farm at Pittsfield. For a term he was a teacher at the common school in the Sykes district. At seventeen he went to sea. Much has been written to account for this, but I cannot see why any further reason need be sought than the one he gives himself: "Sad disappointments in several plans which I had sketched out for my future life; the necessity of doing something for myself, united to a naturally roving disposition, had now conspired within me, to send me to sea as a sailor." He had tried his hand without success at various occupations, and from what we know of his mother we may surmise that she did not hesitate to express her displeasure. He went to sea, as many a boy before and after has done, because he was unhappy at home. Melville was a very strange man, but it is unnecessary to look for strangeness in a perfectly natural proceeding.

He arrived in New York wet through, in patched trousers and a hunting jacket, without a penny in his pocket, but with a fowling piece his brother Gansevoort had given him to sell; walked across town to the house of a friend of his brother's, where he spent the night, and next day with this friend went down to the waterfront. After some search they came across a ship that was sailing for Liverpool, and Melville was signed on as a "boy" at three dollars a month. Twelve years later he wrote in *Redburn* an account of the voyage there and back, and of his stay in Liverpool. He looked upon it as hack-work; but it is vivid and interesting, and it is written in old English that is simple, straightforward, easy and unaffected. It is one of the most readable of his works.

Nothing much is known about how he spent the next three years. According to the accepted accounts he taught school in various places; at one, Greenbush, N. Y., he received six dollars a quarter and board; and he wrote a number of articles for provincial papers. One or two of them have been discovered. They are without interest, but give signs that he had done a lot of desultory reading; and they have a mannerism of which to the end of his life he could never rid himself, namely that of bringing in without rhyme or reason allusions to mythological gods, to historical and romantic characters and to all kinds of authors. As Raymond Weaver neatly puts it: "He called up Burton, Shakespeare, Byron, Milton, Coleridge and Chesterfield, as well as Prometheus and Cinderella, Mahomet and Cleopatra, Madonna and Houris, Medici and Musselman, to strew carelessly across his pages."

But he had an adventurous spirit, and it may be supposed that in the end he could no longer endure the tameness of life to which it seemed circumstances had condemned him. Though he had disliked life before the mast, he made up his mind to go to sea again; and in 1841 he sailed from New Bedford in the whaler *Acushnet* bound for the Pacific. With one exception the men in the forecastle were coarse, brutal and uneducated; the exception was a boy of seventeen called Richard Tobias Greene. This is how Melville describes him: "Toby was endowed with a remarkably prepossessing exterior. Arrayed in his blue frock and duck trousers, he was as smart a looking sailor as ever stepped upon a deck; he was singularly small and slightly made, with great flexibility of limb. His naturally dark complexion had been deepened by exposure to the tropical sun, and a mass of jetty locks clustered about his temples, and threw a darker shade into his large black eyes."

After fifteen months of cruising the *Acushnet* put in at Nukahiva, an island of the Marquesas. The two lads, disgusted with the hardship of life aboard the whaler and the brutality of the captain, decided to desert. They stowed away as much tobacco, ship's biscuit and calico (to give the natives) as they could get into the front of their frocks, and made off for the interior of the island. After several days, during which they had sundry adventures, they reached the valley inhabited by the Typees, and were by them hospitably received. Shortly after their arrival Toby was sent away on the pretext of getting medical help, for Melville on the way had hurt his leg so badly that he could only walk with pain, but in fact to arrange their escape. The Typees were reputed to be cannibals, and prudence suggested that it would be unwise to reckon too long on the continuation of their benevolence. Toby never returned, and it was discovered much later that on arriving at the harbor he had been kidnapped onto a whaler. Melville, by his own account, spent four months in the valley. He was well treated. He made friends with a girl called Fayaway, swam and boated with her, and except for his fear of being eaten was happy enough. Then it happened that the captain of a whaler, putting in at the harbor of Nukahiva, heard that there was a sailor in the hands of the Typees. Many of his own crew having deserted, he sent a boatload of taboo natives to secure the man's release. Melville, again by his own account, persuaded the natives to let him go down to the beach and, after a skirmish in which he killed a man with a boathook, effected his escape.

Life in the ship he now boarded, the *Julia,* was even worse than in the *Acushnet* and on reaching Papeete the crew mutinied. They were held in chains for five days in a French naval vessel and after trial by a tribunal at Papeete consigned to the local jail. The *Julia,* having signed on a new crew, sailed, and the prisoners were in a short time released. With another member of the old crew, a medical man who had come down in the world and whom he calls Doctor Long Ghost, Melville sailed to the neighboring island of Eimeo, and there the pair hired themselves out to two planters to hoe potatoes. Melville hadn't liked farming when he worked for his uncle in Massachusetts, and he liked it still less under the tropical sun of Polynesia. With Doctor Long Ghost he wandered off, living on the natives, and eventually, leaving the doctor behind, persuaded the captain of a whaler which he calls the *Leviathan* to sign him on. In this ship he reached Honolulu. What he did there is uncertain. It is supposed that he found employment as a clerk. Then he shipped as an ordinary seaman in an American frigate, the *United States,* and after a year, upon the ship's arrival home, was discharged from the service.

We have now reached the year 1844. Melville was twenty-five. No portrait of him in youth exists, but from those taken of him in middle age we can picture him in his twenties as a tall, well-set-up man, strong and active, with rather small eyes, but with a straight nose, a fresh color and a fine head of waving hair.

He came home to find his mother and sisters settled at Lansingburg, a suburb of Albany. His elder brother Gansevoort had given up his fur shop and had become a lawyer and a politician; his second brother Allan, a lawyer too, had settled in New York; and his youngest, Tom, soon to go to sea like Herman, was still in his teens.

Herman found himself the center of interest as "the man who had lived among cannibals" and he told the story of his adventures to eager listeners; they urged him to write a book and this forthwith he set out to do.

He had tried his hand at writing before, though with little success, but he had to earn money. When *Typee,* the book in which he described his sojourn on the island of Nukahiva, was finished, Gansevoort Melville, who had gone to London as secretary to the American Minister, submitted it to John Murray, who accepted it, and some time later Wiley and Putnam published it in America. It was well received and Melville, encouraged, wrote the continuation of his adventures in the South Pacific in a book which he called *Omoo.*

It appeared in 1847, and in this year he married Elizabeth, the only daughter of Chief Justice Shaw, whose family had long been known to the Melvilles. The young couple moved to New York, where they lived in Allan Melville's house at 103 Fourth Avenue together with Herman's and Allan's sisters Augusta, Fanny and Helen. We are not told why the three young women left their mother and Lansingburg. Herman settled down to write. In 1849, two years after his marriage, and a few months after the birth of his first child, a boy named Malcolm, he crossed the Atlantic again, this time as a passenger, to see publishers and arrange for the publication of *White Jacket,* the book in which he describes his experiences in the frigate *United States.* From London he went to Paris, Brussels and up the Rhine. His wife wrote as follows in her arid memoir: "Summer of 1849 we remained in New York. He wrote *Redburn* and *White Jacket.* Same fall went to England and published the above. Took little satisfaction in it from mere homesickness, and hurried home, leaving attractive invitations to visit distinguished people—one from the Duke of Rutland to pass a week at Belvoir Castle—see his journal. We went to Pittsfield and boarded in the summer of 1850. Moved to Arrowhead in fall—October 1850."

Arrowhead was the name Melville gave to a farm at Pittsfield which he bought on money advanced by the Chief Justice, and here he settled with his wife, child and sisters. Mrs. Melville in her matter of fact way says in her journal: "Wrote *White Whale* or *Moby Dick* under unfavorable circumstances—would sit at his desk all day not writing anything till four or five o'clock—then ride to the village after dark—would be up early and out walking before breakfast—sometimes splitting wood for exercise. We all felt anxious about the strain on his health in the spring of 1853."

When Melville established himself at Arrowhead he found Hawthorne living in the neighborhood. He took something that very much resembles a schoolgirl crush for the older writer, a crush which may have somewhat disconcerted that reserved, self-centered and undemonstrative man. The letters he wrote to him were impassioned: "I shall leave the world, I feel, with more satisfaction for having come to know you," he said in one of them. "Knowing you persuades me more than the Bible of our immortality." Of an evening he would often ride over to the Red House at Lenox to talk—a little, it appears, to Hawthorne's weariness—of "Providence and futurity and of everything else that lies beyond human ken." While the two authors thus discoursed Mrs. Hawthorne sewed at her stand and in a letter to her mother thus described Melville: * "I am not quite sure that I *do not think him* a very great man . . . A man with a true, warm heart, and a soul and an intellect—with life to his finger tips; earnest, sincere and reverent; very tender *and modest.* . . . He has very keen perceptive power; but what astonishes me is, that his eyes are not large and deep. He seems to see everything very accurately; and how he can do so with his small eyes, I cannot tell. They are not keen eyes, either, but quite undistinguished in any way. His nose is straight and rather handsome, his mouth expressive of sensibility and emotion. He is tall, and erect, with an air free, brave and manly. When conversing, he is full of gesture and force, and loses himself in his subject. There is no grace nor polish. Once in a while, his animation gives place to a singularly quiet expression, out of these eyes to which I have objected; an indrawn, dim look, but which at the same time makes you feel that he is at that moment taking deepest note of what is before him. It is a strange, lazy glance, but with a power in it quite unique. It does not seem to penetrate through you, but to take you into itself." †

* The italics are words underlined by Mrs. Hawthorne.
† Quoted by Raymond Weaver: *Herman Melville, Mariner and Mystic.*

The Hawthornes left Lenox, and the friendship, eager and deep-felt on Melville's side and on Hawthorne's sedate, and perhaps embarrassed, comes to an end. Melville dedicated *Moby Dick* to him. The letter he wrote after reading the book no longer exists, but from Melville's reply it looks as though he guessed that Hawthorne did not like it. Nor did the public, nor did the critics; and *Pierre,* with which he followed it, fared even worse. It was received with contemptuous abuse. He made very little money from his writings, and besides his wife he had two sons and two daughters, and presumably three sisters, to provide for. Melville, judging from his letters, found farming his own land as little to his taste as he had found cutting his uncle's hay at Pittsfield or digging potatoes in Eimeo. The fact is that he had never cared for manual labor: "See my hand!—four blisters on this palm, made by hoes and hammers within the last few days. It is a rainy morning, so I am indoors, and all work suspended. I feel cheerfully disposed . . ." A farmer with hands as soft as that is unlikely to have farmed with profit.

His father-in-law, the Chief Justice, seems periodically to have come to the financial assistance of the family, and as he was a sensible man, besides being evidently a very kind one, it may be supposed that it was he who suggested to Melville that he should look for some other way of earning his living. Various strings were pulled to obtain a consulship for him, but without success, and he was obliged to go on writing. He ailed, and the Chief Justice once more came to the rescue: in 1856 he went abroad again, this time to Constantinople, Palestine, Greece and Italy, and on his return he managed to earn a little money by lecturing. In 1860 he made his last journey. His youngest brother Tom commanded a clipper in the China trade, the *Meteor,* and in this Melville sailed to San Francisco; one would have expected him to have still enough of the spirit of adventure to seize the opportunity to go to the Far East, but for some unknown reason, either because he was bored with his brother or his brother had grown impatient of him, he left the ship at San Francisco and went home. The Chief Justice died. For some years the Melvilles lived in great poverty and in 1863 decided to leave Arrowhead. They bought a house in New York from Allan, Herman's prosperous brother, and in part payment turned Arrow-head over to him. The remainder of the purchase money was raised on mortgage. In this house, 104 East Twenty-sixth Street, Melville lived for the rest of his life.

At this time, according to Raymond Weaver, it was a good year for him if he earned a hundred dollars in royalties on his books; in 1866 he managed to secure an appointment as Inspector of Customs, and the circum-stances of the family grew brighter. In the following year Malcolm, his eldest son, shot himself in his room, but whether by design or accident is not clear; his second son, Stanwick, ran away from home and of him nothing more is heard. Melville held his modest post in the Cus-toms for twenty years; then his wife inherited money from her brother Samuel, and he resigned. In 1878 he published at the expense of his Uncle Gansevoort a poem of twenty thousand lines called *Clarel*. Shortly before his death he wrote, or rewrote, a novelette called *Billy Budd*. He died, forgotten, in 1891. He was seventy-two.

Such in brief is the story of Melville's life as it is told by his biographers, but it is evident that there is much they have not told. They pass over Malcolm's death and Stanwick's flight from home as though they were matters of no consequence. Surely letters must have passed between Mrs. Melville and her brothers when the boy, eighteen years of age, shot himself; one can only suppose that they have been suppressed; it is true that by 1867 Melville's fame had dwindled, but one would expect that such an event would have reminded the press of his existence and some mention would have been made of it in the newspapers. And was there no inquiry into the circumstances of the boy's death? If he committed suicide what made him do so? And why did Stanwick run away? What were the conditions of his life at home that drove him to such a step, and how does it happen that nothing more is heard of him? From the fact that only Mrs. Melville and her two daughters attended Mel-ville's funeral, the only members of his immediate family still alive, we are told, one must suppose that he too was dead. Mrs. Melville, so far as we know, was a good and affectionate mother: it is strange that, again so far as we know, she seems to have taken no steps to get in touch with her only remaining son. The records show that in his old age Melville was fond of his grandchildren, but his feeling for his own children is ambiguous. Lewis Mumford, whose biography of Melville is sensible, and to all appearance trustworthy, gives a grim picture of his relations with them. He seems to have been a harsh, impatient father and to have teased them unkindly: "One of his daughters could not recur to the image of her father without a certain painful revulsion. . . . When he purchased a work of art, a print or a statue for ten dollars, when there was scarcely bread to go round who can wonder at their black memories?" He had, it appears, a jocularity which was little to their taste, and if you read between the lines, you can hardly escape the suspicion that he sometimes came home the worse for liquor. For this, I hasten to add, there is no direct evidence. But there is little evidence for anything to confirm any view one may take of his character; and one does no more than surmise when one decides that he was selfish, work-shy and shiftless.

What occasioned the change from the man who wrote *Typee* and *Omoo* to the man who wrote *Moby Dick* and *Pierre* and who, when barely more than thirty, was written out? I have found *Omoo* more readable than *Typee*. It is a straightforward narrative of Melville's experiences on the island of Eimeo and on the whole may be accepted as true. *Typee,* on the other hand, seems to be a hotchpotch of fact and fancy. According to Charles Roberts Anderson, Melville spent only a month on the island of Nukahiva and not four as he pretended, and his adventures on his way to the valley of the Typees were not so startling as he makes out nor the dangers he ran from their supposed predilection for human flesh so great; and the story of his escape, as he gives it, is highly improbable: ". . . the whole scene of the rescue itself is romantic and unconvincing, apparently written in haste and more with a view to making himself a hero than with a proper regard to logic and dramatic finesse." Melville should not be blamed for this; we know that he repeatedly gave an account of his adventures to willing listeners, and everyone knows how hard it is to resist the temptation of making a story a little better and a little more exciting each time you tell it. It would have been embarrassing for him when he came to write it to state the sober and not peculiarly thrilling facts when in numberless talks he had freely embroidered upon them.

Typee, in fact, appears to be a compilation of matter which Melville found in contemporary travel books combined with a highly colored version of his own experiences. The industrious Mr. Anderson has shown that he on occasion not only repeated the errors these travel books contained, but in various instances used the very words of their authors. I think this accounts for a certain heaviness the reader may find in it. But both *Typee* and *Omoo* are well enough written in the idiom of the period. Melville was already inclined to use the literary word rather than the plain one: so, for example, he prefers to call a building an *edifice*; one hut isn't near another or even in its neighborhood, but in the *vicinity*; he is more apt to be *fatigued* than like most people, tired; and he prefers to *evince* rather than to show feeling.

But the portrait of the author of both these books emerges clearly, and you need make no imaginative effort to see that he was a hardy, grave and determined young man, high-spirited and fond of fun, work-shy but not lazy; gay, amiable, friendly and carefree. He was charmed with the prettiness of the Polynesian girls, as any young fellow of his age would be, and it would be strange if he did not accept the favors they were certainly willing to grant him. If there was anything unusual in him it was that he took a keen delight in beauty, something to which youth is apt to be indifferent, and there is some intensity in his admiring description of the sea and the sky and the green mountains. Perhaps the only indication there is that there was more in him than in any other sailor man of three and twenty is that he was of a pondering turn, and conscious of it. "I am of a meditative humour," he wrote much later, "and at sea used often to mount aloft at night, and, seating myself in one of the upper yards, tuck my jacket about me and give loose to reflection."

How is one to account for the transformation of this apparently normal young man into the savage pessimist who wrote *Pierre?* What turned the commonplace, undistinguished writer of *Typee* into the darkly imaginative, powerful, inspired and eloquent author of *Moby Dick?* Well, in these days of sex-consciousness we look for sexual causes to explain strange circumstances.

Typee and *Omoo* were written before Melville married Elizabeth Shaw. During the first year of their union he wrote *Mardi*. It begins as a straightforward continuation of his adventures before the mast, but then it becomes wildly fanciful. It is long-winded and to my mind tedious. I cannot put its theme better than has been done by Raymond Weaver: *"Mardi* is a quest after some total and undivided possession of that holy and mysterious joy that touched Melville during the period of his courtship: a joy he had felt in the crucifixion of his love for his mother; a joy that had dazzled him in his love for Elizabeth Shaw. . . . And *Mardi* is a pilgrimage for a lost glamour. . . . It is a quest after Yillah, a maiden from Oroolia, the Island of Delight. A voyage is made through the civilized world for her: and though they (the persons of the novel) find occasion for much discourse on international politics, and an array of other topics, Yillah is not found."

If one wants to indulge in conjecture one may take this strange story as the first sign of his disappointment with the married state. One has to guess what Elizabeth Shaw, Mrs. Melville, was like from the few letters of hers that remain. She was not a good letter-writer, and it may be that there was more in her than they reveal; but they show at least that she was in love with her husband and that she was a sensible, kindly, practical, though perhaps narrow and conventional, woman. She bore poverty without complaint. She was doubtless puzzled by her husband's development and perhaps regretful that he seemed bent on throwing away the reputation and popularity *Typee* and *Omoo* had won him, but she continued to believe in him and to admire him to the end. She was not a woman of intellect, but she was a good, tolerant and affectionate wife.

Did he love her? No letters that he may have written during his courtship remain. He married her. But men don't marry only for love. It may be that he had had enough of a wandering life and wanted to settle down: one of the strange things about this strange man is that though, as he says himself, of "a naturally roving disposition," after his first journey as a boy to Liverpool and his three years in the South Seas, his thirst for adventure was quenched. Such journeys as he took later were mere tourist trips. It may be that Melville married because his family and friends thought it was high time he did, or it may be that he married in order to combat inclinations that dismayed him. Who can tell? Lewis Mumford says that "he was never quite happy in Elizabeth's company, nor was he quite happy away from it," and suggests that he felt not merely affection for her, but "on these long absences, passion would gather within him," only to be followed by quick satiety. He would not have been the first man to find that he loves his wife more when he is parted from her than when he is with her, and that the expectation of sexual intercourse is more exciting than the realization. I think it is probable that Melville was impatient with the marriage tie; it may be that his wife gave him less than he had hoped, but he continued to have marital relations long enough for her to bear him four children. He remained so far as anyone knows faithful to her.

I have not yet in this essay dealt with *Pierre*. It is a preposterous book. Of course there are in it pregnant sayings: Melville wrote in pain and bitterness, and his passion from time to time gave rise to passages that are powerful and eloquent; but the incidents are improbable, the motives unconvincing and the conversations bombastic. *Pierre* might be the invention of a schoolgirl of fourteen who had nourished her neurotic mind on the worst kind of romantic fiction. Indeed, it gives one the impression that it was written in a condition of advanced neurasthenia. But the book has proved a treasure to the psychoanalysts, and to them I am glad to leave it.

I wonder, however, what the psychoanalysts would say to the fact that in the lecture Melville gave on sculpture after his return from Palestine and Italy he should have singled out for special comment the Greco-Roman statue called the Apollo Belvedere. It is a dull, uninspired production, and its only merit is that it represents a very handsome young man. Melville had an eye for masculine beauty. I have already described the impression made on him by Toby, the boy in whose company he deserted the *Acushnet*, and in *Typee* he remarks more than once on the physical perfection of the young men with whom he consorted. It will be remembered that at the age of seventeen he sailed in a ship bound for Liverpool. There he made friends with a boy whom he calls Harry Bolton. This is how he describes him in *Redburn*: "He was one of those small, but perfectly formed beings with curling hair, and silken muscles, who seem to have been born in cocoons. His complexion was a mantling brunet, feminine as a girl's; his feet were small, his hands very white; and his eyes were large, black and womanly; and, poetry aside, his voice was as the sound of a harp." Doubt has been thrown on the hurried jaunt the two boys made to London, which certainly reads very unconvincingly, and even on the existence of such a person as Harry Bolton; but if Melville invented him to add an interesting episode to his book, it is odd that so manly a fellow as he should have invented a character who was so obviously homosexual.

In the frigate *United States* Melville's great friend was an English sailor, Jack Chase, "tall and well-knit, with a clear open eye, a fine broad brow, and an abounding nut-brown beard." "There was such an abounding air of good sense and good feeling about the man," he wrote in *White Jacket,* "that he who could not love him, would thereby pronounce himself a knave"; and further: "Wherever you may be now rolling over the blue billows, dear Jack, take my best love with you, and God bless you, wherever you go." A touch of tenderness which is rare in Melville! So deep an impression did this sailor make on Melville that he dedicated to him the novelette, *Billy Budd,* which he completed only three months before his death fifty years later. The story hangs on the hero's amazing beauty. It is this that causes everyone in the ship to love him, and it is this that indirectly brings about his tragic end.

I have dwelt on this trait in Melville's character because it is just possible that it may account for his dissatisfaction with married life, and it may be that a sexual frustration occasioned the change in him which has puzzled all who have interested themselves in him. I think the probabilities are that he was a very moral man; but who can tell what instincts, perhaps even unrecognized, and if recognized angrily repressed and never, except perhaps in imagination, indulged in, who can tell, I say, what instincts may dwell in a man's being which, though never yielded to, may yet have an overwhelming effect on his disposition?

It has been suggested that the peculiar transformation in Melville's character, which turned the author of *Typee* into the author of *Moby Dick,* was occasioned by an attack of insanity. But that he was ever out of his mind

has been as hotly denied by his admirers as if it were
something disgraceful; it is of course no more disgraceful
than to have an attack of jaundice. In any case, if there
is any evidence of it, it has not, so far as I know, been
produced. It has been suggested also that Melville was
so profoundly affected as to become a different man by
the intensive reading he undertook when he moved from
Lansingburg to New York; the notion that he was crazed
by Sir Thomas Browne as Don Quixote was crazed by
romances of chivalry carries no conviction. It is too naive.
It may be that the mystery will be cleared up if ever
research uncovers further documents, but at present it
must remain unexplained. In some unknown way the
commonplace writer became a writer of something very
like genius.

Melville's reading, though desultory, had always been
wide. It is plain that he was chiefly attracted by the poets
and prose writers of the seventeenth century, and one
must presume that he found in them something that
peculiarly accorded with his own confused proclivities.
Whether their influence was harmful to him or beneficial
is a matter of personal opinion. His early education was
slight and, as often happens in such cases, he did not
quite assimilate the culture he acquired in later years.
Culture is not something you put on like a ready-made
suit of clothes, but a nourishment you absorb to build
up your personality, just as food builds up the body of
the growing boy. It is not an ornament used to decorate
a phrase, still less to show off your knowledge, but a
means, painfully acquired, to enrich the soul.

Robert Louis Stevenson claimed that Melville had no
ear: I should have said on the contrary that his ear was
very sensitive. Though he spelled erratically and his
grammar was sometimes faulty, he had a wonderful sense
of rhythm, and the balance of his sentences, however
long, is excellent. He liked the high-sounding phrase, and
the stately vocabulary he employed enabled him frequently to get effects of great beauty. Sometimes this inclination led him to tautology, as when he speaks of the
"umbrageous shade," which only means the shady shade;
but one can scarcely deny that the sound is rich. Sometimes one is pulled up by such a tautology as "hasty
precipitancy" only to discover with some awe that Milton
wrote: "Thither they hasted with glad precipitance."

Sometimes Melville uses common words in an unexpected way and often obtains by this means a pleasant novelty of effect; and even when it seems to you that he has used them in a meaning they cannot bear, it is rash to blame him "with hasty precipitancy," for he may well have authority to go on. When he speaks of "redundant hair," it may occur to you that hair may be redundant on a maiden's lip, but hardly on a young man's head; but if you look it up in the dictionary you will find that the second sense of redundant is copious, and Milton (Milton again!) wrote of "redundant locks."

I sympathize less with Melville's liking for archaic words and words only in poetic usage; *o'er* for over; *nigh* for near, *ere* for before; *anon* and *eftsoons* give a fusty, meretricious air to prose that is solid and virile. I think there is greater excuse for his partiality for the second person singular. It is an awkward mode of speech and presumably for that reason has fallen into disuse, but I can well believe that Melville employed it to achieve the deliberate purpose he had in view. He may have felt that it gave something of a hieratic turn to the conversations he reported and a poetic flavor to the words used.

But these are trifles. Whatever reservations one may make, Melville wrote English uncommonly well. His style reached its perfection in *Moby Dick*. Sometimes, of course, the manner he had acquired led him to rhetorical extravagance, but at its best it has a copious magnificence, a sonority, a grandeur, an eloquence that no modern writer, so far as I know, has achieved. It does indeed often recall the majestic phrase of Sir Thomas Browne and the stately period of Milton. I cannot leave this side of my subject without calling the reader's attention to the ingenuity with which Melville wove into the elaborate pattern of his prose the ordinary nautical terms used by sailor men in the course of their daily work. The effect is to bring a note of realism, the savor of the fresh salt of the sea, to the somber symphony which is the unique novel of *Moby Dick*.

No one who has ever read a word I have written will expect me to speak of *Moby Dick*, Melville's great achievement and his only title to rank with the great writers of fiction, from the esoteric and allegorical side. Readers must go elsewhere for that. I can only deal with it from my own standpoint of a not inexperienced novelist.

But since some very intelligent persons have taken *Moby Dick* for an allegory it is proper that I should deal with the matter. They have regarded as ironical Melville's own remark; he feared, he wrote, that his work might be looked upon "as a monstrous fable, or still worse and more detestable, a hideous and intolerable allegory." Is it rash to assume that when a practiced writer says a thing, he is more likely to mean what he says than what his commentators think he means? It is true that in a letter to Mrs. Hawthorne he remarked that he had while writing "some vague idea that the whole book was susceptible of an allegorical construction"; but that is slender evidence that he had the intention of writing an allegory. May it not be possible that if it is indeed susceptible to such an interpretation, it is something that came about by accident and, as his words to Mrs. Hawthorne seem to indicate, not a little to his surprise? I don't know how critics write novels, but I have some notion how novelists write them. They do not take a general proposition such as Honesty is the Best Policy or All is not Gold that Glitters; and say: Let's write an allegory about that. A group of characters, generally suggested by persons they have known, excites their imagination, and sometimes simultaneously, sometimes after a time an incident or a string of incidents experienced, heard or invented appears out of the blue to enable them to make suitable use of them in the development of the theme that has arisen in their minds by a sort of collaboration between the characters and incidents. Melville was not fanciful, or at least when he attempted the fanciful, as in *Mardi,* he came a cropper. To imagine, and his imagination was powerful, he needed a solid basis of fact. When, as in *Pierre,* he gave it a free rein without this basis he wrote absurdly. It is true that he was of a "pondering" turn, and as he grew older he became absorbed in metaphysics, which Raymond Weaver states is "but misery dissolved in thought." That is a narrow way of putting it: there is no subject to which man can more fitly give his attention, for it deals with the greatest problems that confront his soul: value, God, immortality and the meaning of life. Melville's approach to these questions was not intellectual, but emotional: he thought as he did because he felt as he did; but this does not prevent many of his reflections from being profound. *"Le coeur a ses raisons que la raison ne connaît point."* I should have thought that deliberately to write an allegory required an intellectual detachment of which Melville was incapable.

No one has gone further than Ellery Sedgwick in the symbolic interpretation of *Moby Dick*. He goes so far as to claim that its symbolism is what makes the book great. According to him Ahab is "Man—man sentient, speculative, purposive, religious, standing his full stature against the immense mystery of creation. His antagonist, Moby Dick, is that immense mystery. He is not the author of it, but is identical with that galling impartiality in the laws and lawlessness of the universe which Isaiah devoutly fathered on the Creator." I find this hard to believe. A more plausible interpretation is given by Lewis Mumford in his biography of Melville. If I understand him aright he takes Moby Dick as a symbol of Evil, and Ahab's conflict with him as the conflict of Good and Evil in which Good is finally vanquished; and this accords well with Melville's moody pessimism. But allegories are awkward animals to handle; you can take them by the head or by the tail, and I would suggest that another interpretation is equally plausible.

Why have the commentators assumed that Moby Dick is a symbol of evil? The "empty malice" of which Professor Mumford speaks consists in his defending himself when he is attacked.

> *"Cet animal est très méchant,*
> *Quand on l'attaque, il se défend."*

Let us remember that *Typee* is a glorification of the noble savage uncorrupted by the vices of civilization. Melville looked upon the natural man as good. Why should the White Whale not represent goodness rather than evil? Splendid in beauty, vast in size, great in strength, he swims the seas in freedom. Captain Ahab with his insane pride is pitiless, harsh, cruel and revengeful; *he* is Evil; and when the final encounter comes, Ahab and his crew of "mongrel renegades, castaways and cannibals" are destroyed, and the White Whale, imperturbable, justice having been done, goes his mysterious way; evil has been vanquished and good at last triumphed. Or if you want another interpretation on the same lines you might

take Ahab with his dark wickedness for Satan and the
White Whale for his Creator. Then when God, though
wounded to the death, has destroyed the Evil One, Ish-
mael—man—is left to float on the "soft and dirge-like
main" with nothing more to hope or fear, alone with his
unconquerable soul.

Fortunately *Moby Dick* may be read, and read with
passionate interest, without a thought of what allegorical
significance it may or may not have. I cannot repeat
too often that a novel is to be read not for instruction
or edification but for intelligent enjoyment, and if you
find you cannot get this from it you had far better not
read it at all. But it must be admitted that Melville
seems to have done his best to hinder his reader's enjoyment. "What I feel more moved to write," he said
in one of his letters, "that is banned—it will not pay.
Yet, altogether write the other way I cannot." He was
of an obstinate temper, and it may be that the neglect
of the public, the savage onslaughts of the critics and
the lack of understanding in those nearest to him only
confirmed him in his determination to write exactly as
he chose. Montgomery Belgion in a judicious introduction to a recent edition of *Moby Dick* has supposed that
since it is a tale of pursuit and the end of the pursuit
must be perpetually delayed, Melville wrote the chapters
dealing with the natural history of the whale, its size,
skeleton and whatnot, to do this. I don't believe it. If
he had any such purpose during the three years he spent
in the Pacific he must surely have witnessed incidents
or been told tales that he could have used more fitly to
effect it. I should have said that Melville wrote these
particular chapters for the simple reason that he could
not resist bringing into the work he was writing any
piece of information that interested him. For my part I
can read them all with interest except that which deals
with the whiteness of the whale. To my mind that is absurd. But it cannot be denied that they are digressions
which impede the narrative. There is one other point
which may cause the reader a sense of disappointment
and this is Melville's way of describing a character at
length and then dropping him: you have been fascinated
by him, you want to know more about him but you are
left at a loose end. The fact is that Melville hadn't got
what the French call *l'esprit de suite,* and it would be

stupid to assert that his novel is well constructed. If he composed *Moby Dick* in the way he did, it is because that is how he wanted it. You must take it or leave it. He would not be the first novelist to say: "Well, I might write a more satisfactory book if I did this, that or the other as you suggest, I daresay you're perfectly right, but this is how I like it and this is how I'm going to do it, and if other people don't like it I can't help it, and what's more, I don't care."

Some critics have accused Melville of lacking invention, but I think without reason. It is true that he invented more convincingly when he had a substratum of experience to sustain him; but then so do most novelists, and when he had this his imagination worked freely and with power. I have little more to say. It is hardly worth while to point out, for it cannot escape the most careless reader's attention, that when Melville has action to describe he does it magnificently, with great force, and his somewhat formal manner of writing curiously enhances the thrilling effect. The early chapters, when the scene is laid in New Bedford, are intensely real and at the same time enchantingly romantic. They beautifully prepare the mind for what is to come after. But of course it is the sinister and gigantic figure of Captain Ahab that pervades the book and gives it its emotional quality. I can think of no creature of fiction that approaches his stature. You must go to the Greek dramatists for anything like that sense of doom with which everything that you are told about him fills you, and to Shakespeare to find beings of such terrible power. It is because Herman Melville created him that, notwithstanding all the reservations one may make, *Moby Dick* is a great, a very great book.

POSTSCRIPT

EACH OF THE ESSAYS in this book was written with the sole purpose of telling the reader something about the particular novel he was invited to read, and since it is natural to want to know what sort of persons they were that wrote such books as these I have added some account of their authors. I could allow myself only a severely limited space, so that in dealing with the life and character of each one I have confined myself to what seemed to me significant facts. I have mentioned the various books from which I learned them, and to such of their authors as are still living I here tender my thanks for the instruction and entertainment they have afforded me.

During the year and more that I have spent reading again the novels which are included in the series for which my introductions were designed, and studying the lives of their writers, a number of reflections have from time to time occurred to me concerning the general characteristics of the authors and their books. I could not but ask myself what it was that these great authors had that made them what they were, and what it was in these books that has made them of enduring interest to a long succession of readers. The conclusions I have come to, and the answers to my questions, are tentative, and I beg the reader to take them as such. I can only generalize, and no generalization can have more than a very partial truth. Moreover, in the present case, I am generalizing on a small number of instances.

All these books have been bestsellers. It is true that three of them, namely *The Red and the Black, Wuthering Heights* and *Moby Dick*, were dead failures when first published. Such critics as noticed them had little good to say of them. The public ignored them. That is easy to understand. They were highly original. Now, the world in general doesn't know what to make of originality; it is startled out of its comfortable habits of thought, and its first reaction is one of anger. It needs a long time, and the guidance of perceptive interpreters, before it can abandon its instinctive recoil and accustom itself to novelty. Take, for example, the Impressionist School of painters, of which the most important members were Monet, Manet and Renoir. It is almost incredible that when they were first painted their pictures were received with howls of execration. Now we can see nothing startling in them, and we wonder that the people who first saw them shouldn't have seen at once the beauties that are so manifest to us. We are told that these painters had difficulty in selling for a few hundred francs works of art which are sold now for many thousand dollars, and we think what a chance we have missed, since if we'd been alive then we might have bought for next to nothing pictures that we should be proud to possess. But of course we should have done nothing of the kind. We should have thought them as preposterous as everyone else did. It needed long years of acquaintance to enable us to reconcile ourselves to the new aspect of nature which these painters perceived and set down on canvas.

So it has been with the three books I have mentioned. Let us not forget that when Stendhal wanted to reissue his works, his most intimate friend, a man of education and considerable culture, begged him to leave out *The Red and the Black*. Charlotte Brontë, when a new edition of her sister's *Wuthering Heights* was called for, largely on account of the reputation she had herself made, felt bound to apologize for it. Hawthorne, it is evident, notwithstanding his friendship with Melville, and his admiration for his character, was disconcerted by *Moby Dick*.

But time has changed all that. The outstanding merits of these three novels have long been recognized. They have become bestsellers. As for the other novels I have dealt with, their success with the public was instantaneous. They were bestsellers from the day of their publication and have remained so ever since.

I have dwelt upon this matter in order to point out how stupid it is of a certain class of critics, and unhappily also of a portion of the public that regards itself as belonging to the intelligentsia, to condemn a book because it is a bestseller. It is inept to suppose that a book that vast numbers of people want to read, and so buy, is necessarily worse than a book that very few people want to read, and so don't buy. Logan Pearsall Smith, with a comfortable income of his own derived from a bottle factory and a cemetery that belonged to his family, wrote: "The writer who writes for money does not write for me." It was a very silly remark, which only showed his ignorance of literary history. Dr. Johnson, who said that: "No man but a blockhead ever wrote, except for money," wrote one of the minor masterpieces of English literature to get enough money to pay for his mother's funeral. Balzac and Dickens without shame wrote for money. The critic's business is to judge the book he is concerned with on its merits. The motives for which the author wrote it have nothing to do with him, any more than has the number of copies it has sold. But if he is a thoughtful critic he may find it interesting to trace the variety of motives which may result in the production of a work of art and to inquire into what are the peculiar characteristics that make a book of interest to great masses of people of various degrees of cultivation and enlightenment. In this connection he might find it useful to compare *David Copperfield* with *Gone with the Wind* and *War and Peace* with *Uncle Tom's Cabin.*

Of course I do not mean that a bestseller is necessarily a good book. It may be a very bad one. A book may become a bestseller because it deals with a subject that at the time happens to interest the public, and so notwithstanding the great faults it may have is widely read. When the public ceases to be interested in this particular subject the book is forgotten. A book may become a bestseller because it is pornographic, there is always a public for dirt, and should the publisher and the author be so fortunate as to get the advertisement of public prosecution the sales may be large indeed. A book may become a bestseller because it satisfies the desire for adventure and romance in the many people who by circumstances are deprived of both. It is ungenerous to grudge them their only means of escape from the monotony and loneliness of their lives. In America of late years intensive advertisement has vastly increased the sales of books, both of fiction and non-fiction, and this has often happened with books of very little value, but I think all publishers will agree that, however much money they may be prepared to spend in publicity, they can never succeed in getting a book widely read unless there is in it something to appeal to the public. All their advertisements can do is to bring it to the attention of the people who will enjoy reading it.

That they may do this, though it may be badly constructed, badly written, commonplace, pretentious, sentimental and improbable, it must have something to make it readable. It must have an appeal to something common to the great mass of mankind. That can only mean that it has at least some merit. It is no use saying that people should not like a book that has such great defects. They do; they remain indifferent to them because they are taken with the particular something that they find in the book. It would be useful if the critics pointed out what this something is. So they would instruct us.

When I come to consider what are the characteristics that have made these ten novels with which I have been dealing persistently popular I am first of all confronted with the fact that they are all very different from one another. All have their merits and all have their defects. Some of them are badly written, some are badly constructed, some are scarcely plausible, some are long-winded, at least one is sentimental, another is brutal. But one point they have in common: they have absorbing stories. You want to know how things will turn out; and you want to know this because you are interested in the characters the authors have invented. You are interested in them because you accept them as real people, however unlike those you happen to know, and you accept them as such, even Mr. Micawber, because their creators have seen them vividly and invested them with idiosyncrasy. They have inspired them with their own vitality. And the subjects the authors treat are the subjects of enduring interest to human beings: God, love and hate, death, money, ambition, envy, pride, good and evil. They have in short dealt with the passions and instincts and desires common to us all. They have honestly tried to tell the truth, but they have seen it through the distorting lens of their own unusual personalities. It is because they have dealt with the subjects that concern men from age to age that from generation to generation men have found in their books something to their purpose; and it is because they have seen life, judged it and described it, as their unusual personalities revealed it to them, that their books have the tang, the individuality, which continues so powerfully to attract us. In the final analysis all the author has to give you is himself, and it is because in their diverse ways these several authors had personalities of peculiar force and of great singularity that their books, notwithstanding the passage of time, bringing with it different habits of life and new ways of thought, retain their fascination.

There is another point common to them which I think worth taking note of. These authors have told their stories in a very straightforward manner; they have narrated events, delved into motives and described emotions without recourse to any of the "literary" tricks which make so many modern novels tedious. It does not appear that they ever sought to impress by their subtlety or to startle by their originality. As men they are complicated enough, but as writers they are astonishingly simple. They are subtle and original as naturally as Monsieur Jourdain spoke prose.

I was curious to discover, if I could, whether there was anything common to these several authors by means of which I could gain some notion of the characteristics which enabled them to write books to which the consensus of qualified opinion has agreed to ascribe greatness. Little is known either of Fielding, Jane Austen or Emily Brontë, but as regards the others the material for such an enquiry is overwhelming. Stendhal and Tolstoy wrote volume after volume about themselves; Flaubert's revealing correspondence is enormous; and of the rest friends and relations have written reminiscences and biographers elaborate lives.

Of course there is in everyone something of the creative instinct. It is natural for a child to play about with colored pencils and paint little pictures in water colors, and then, when it learns to read and write, to write little verses and little stories. Since at first sight it seems easier to write than to paint the child as it grows older is more apt to devote itself to writing. It is evidently more amusing to invent than to copy. I have a belief that the creative instinct reaches its height during the twenties and then, sometimes because it was merely a product of adolescence, sometimes because the affairs of life, the necessity of earning a living, leave no time for its exercise, it languishes and dies. But in many people, in more than most of us know, it continues to burden or enchant them. They become writers because of the compulsion within them. But unfortunately you may have the creative instinct strongly developed and yet not have the capacity to create anything of interest.

What is it that must be combined with the creative instinct to enable a writer to produce work of value? Well, I suppose it is personality. It is an idiosyncrasy he possesses that enables him to see in a manner peculiar to himself. It may be a pleasant or an unpleasant personality. That doesn't matter. Nor does it matter if he sees in a way that common opinion regards as neither just nor true. The only thing that matters is that he should see with his own eyes, and that his eyes should show him a world peculiar to himself. You may not like the world he sees, the world, for instance, that Stendhal or Flaubert saw, and then his work will be distasteful to you, but you can hardly fail to be impressed by the force with which he has presented it; or you may like his world, as you like the world of Fielding, Jane Austen and Dickens, and then you will take him to your heart. That depends on your own temperament. It has nothing to do with the value of his work.

I don't think anyone who has read what I have had to say about these ten authors can have failed to notice that they were all persons of marked and unusual individuality. Of course they all had the creative instinct strongly developed, and they all had a passion for writing. If one may judge by these examples, one may safely say that it is not much of a writer who hates writing. That is not to say that they didn't find it difficult. It is not easy to write well. No one writes as well as he would like to; he only writes as well as he can. Flaubert, the reader will remember, found it a fearful task to satisfy himself; and both Tolstoy and Balzac wrote, rewrote and corrected almost endlessly. But still, to write was their passion. It was not only the business of their lives, but a need as exigent as hunger or thirst.

They were none of them highly educated. Flaubert and Tolstoy were great readers, but chiefly to obtain material for what they wanted to write; the others were no more widely read than the average person of the class they belonged to. Nor do they seem to have taken much interest in arts other than their own. Tolstoy was fond of music and played the piano, and Stendhal had a predilection for opera, which is the form of musical entertainment which affords pleasure to people who don't like music. I have not discovered that it meant much to any of the rest. Nor did the plastic arts. Such references as you find in their books to painting or sculpture indicate that their taste was distressingly conventional. They were not very intelligent. I don't mean by this that they were stupid; it requires intelligence to write a good novel, but not of a very high order. Their naïveté when they deal with general ideas is often startling. They accept the commonplaces of the current philosophy of their day, and when they put them to use in their fiction the result is seldom happy. The fact is, ideas are not their business; and their concern with them, when they *are* concerned with them, is emotional. They have little gift for conceptual thought. They are not interested in the proposition, but in the example, for it is the concrete that interests them. Tell them that all men are mortal and they remain cold, but go on to say that Socrates is a man, and they will sit up and take notice. But if intelligence is not their strong point, they make up for it with gifts that are more useful to them. They feel strongly, even passionately; they have imagination, keen observation, and an ability to put themselves in the shoes of the characters of their invention and to rejoice in their joys and suffer with their pains; and finally they have a faculty for giving body and shape to what they have seen, felt and imagined. For they have seen, felt and imagined with extraordinary force and distinctness.

But before proceeding with these observations I must deal with the exceptional cases of Emily Brontë and Dostoevsky. It is an abnormal thing for the creative instinct to possess a person after the age of thirty, and so in some respects all these writers were abnormal; but with an abnormality that was natural to their gifts; the abnormality of Emily Brontë and of Dostoevsky was the outcome of adventitious circumstances. Emily Brontë suffered from a shyness so severe as to be pathological, and, I surmise, from unrecognized sexual inclinations; while Dostoevsky was an epileptic. Flaubert also suffered from this disease, but he was free from it for years at a time, and its effects on his character were mitigated by his strength of will and native good sense. This brings me to a notion that has been put forward that a physical disability or an unhappy experience in childhood is the determining source of the creative instinct. Thus Byron would never have become a poet if he had not had a clubfoot, and Dickens would never have become a novelist if he had not spent a few weeks in a blacking factory. This is nonsense. Innumerable men have been born with a malformed foot, innumerable children have been put to work they found ignominious, without ever writing ten lines of verse or prose. The creative instinct is common to all men; in a privileged number it is vigorous and persistent; neither Byron with his clubfoot, Dostoevsky with his epilepsy, nor Dickens with his unfortunate experience at the blacking factory, would have become a writer at all unless he had had the urge from the composition of his own nature. It is the same urge as possessed the healthy Henry Fielding, the healthy Jane Austen and the healthy Tolstoy. I have no doubt that a physical or spiritual disability (in Dickens' case a vulgar snobbishness) affects the character of an author's work. To some extent it sets him apart from his fellows, it makes him miserably self-conscious, it prejudices him, so that he sees the world, life and his fellow creatures from a standpoint, often unduly pessimistic, which is not the usual one; and more than all, it adds introversion to the extroversion with which the creative instinct is inexorably associated. I don't doubt that Dostoevsky would not have written the sort of books he wrote if he hadn't been an epileptic, but neither do I doubt that in that case he would still have been the voluminous writer he was.

But now setting aside these sick creatures to consider the others, I think the first thing that must strike one is that they had immense vitality.

It is a mistake to suppose that the creative artist likes to live in a garret. He doesn't. There is an exuberance in his nature that leads him to display. He relishes luxury. He loves having a good time. Remember Fielding with his hunters and his lackeys in gaudy liveries, Stendhal with his fine clothes, his cabriolet and his groom, Balzac with his senseless ostentation, Dickens with his grand dinner parties, his fine house, and his carriage and pair. There was nothing of the ascetic about them. They had a prodigious power of enjoyment, and liked the good things of life. They wanted money, not to hoard it, but to fling it away with both hands, and they were not always scrupulous in the way they got it. But if they were madly extravagant, they were also open-handed; they would take money from any source open to them and give to anyone in need of it. They had great nervous energy. They were good company and great talkers, and their charm seems to have impressed everyone who came in contact with them.

Some of them died young, Emily Brontë from the tuberculosis that affected her entire family, Jane Austen owing to a feminine malady which could today probably have been cured, Fielding owing to the dissipation of his youth and Balzac owing to overwork and his unhealthy mode of living; but taking into consideration the time allotted to them, they produced, with the exception of Emily Brontë who only wrote one book and a few poems, a great body of work. It should be remembered that Jane Austen's writing life extended to less than ten years. They worked hard, and from such accounts as have come down to us of their habits of work it appears that they adopted a methodical routine. Not for them was the Bohemian's plea that he can only write when he feels "in the mood," or when "the spirit moves him"; however loose and unconventional their lives were, when it came to writing they went to their desks as regularly as the shipping clerk goes to his office. One cannot but be impressed by their industry.

They had, however, other traits which were less commendable. They were extremely self-centered. Nothing really mattered to them but their work, and to this they were prepared to sacrifice without a qualm everyone connected with them. They were inconsiderate, selfish and pig-headed. They had little self-control, and it never occurred to them not to gratify a whim because it might bring distress to others. They do not seem to have been much inclined to marry, and when they did, either on account of their natural irritability or on account of their inconstancy, they brought their wives scant happiness. I

think they married as a means of escape from the hurly-
burly of their agitating instincts: to settle down seemed
to offer them peace and rest, and they thought that marriage was an anchorage where they could live safe from
the stormy waves of the tempestuous world. But escape,
peace and rest, safety, were the last things to suit their
temperaments. Marriage is an affair of perpetual compromise, and how could they be expected to compromise
when egoism was of the essence of their natures? They
had love affairs, but they do not appear to have been
very satisfactory either to themselves or to the objects
of their volatile affections. And that is understandable:
real love surrenders, real love is selfless, real love is
tender; but tenderness, selflessness and self-surrender
were not virtues of which they were capable. With the
exception of the eminently normal Fielding and the
lecherous Tolstoy they do not appear to have been highly sexed. One suspects that when they had love affairs
it was more to gratify their vanity or to prove to themselves their own virility then because they were carried
off their feet by an irresistible attraction. I venture to
guess that when they had achieved these objects they
returned to their work with a sigh of relief.

Now all this is very rough and ready. I have left out
of consideration the environment and the climate of
opinion in which my authors passed their lives, and yet
it is certain that their influence on them was far from
negligible. With the exception of *Tom Jones,* the novels
of which I have treated appeared in the nineteenth century. That was a period of revolution, social, industrial
and political; men abandoned modes of life and ways of
thought which had prevailed with little change for generations. It may be that such a period, when old beliefs
are no longer unquestioningly accepted, when there is
a great ferment in the air and life is a new and exciting
adventure, is conducive to the production of exceptional
characters and of exceptional works; but I have neither
the space nor the necessary knowledge to deal with the
complicated subject.

I have chosen a few persons about whom I have
learned something and made general statements about
them which in the case of one or another might easily
be shown to have no foundation. We know little about
Jane Austen, but from what we do, I am prepared to

PREMIER WORLD CLASSICS

CELEBRATED MASTERPIECES OF FICTION SELECTED AND
PRESENTED UNDER THE EDITORIAL DIRECTION OF DR.
BERGEN EVANS, NOTED EDUCATOR AND AUTHOR.

THE AMBASSADORS—by Henry James—#D88—50¢

ARMANCE—by Stendhal—#D101—50¢

CONSUELO—by George Sand—#T125—75¢

DOMBEY AND SON—by Charles Dickens—#M184—95¢

ESTHER WATERS—by George Moore—#D95—50¢

FAR FROM THE MADDING CROWD—by Thomas Hardy—
#D106—50¢

GIL BLAS—by Alain René le Sage—A modern abridgment
—#T157—75¢

I PROMESSI SPOSI (THE BETROTHED)—by Alessandro Man-
zoni—A modern abridgment—#M176—95¢

THE KREUTZER SONATA—by Leo Tolstoy—Newly translated by Beatrice Scott—#D121—50¢

LES MISÉRABLES—by Victor Hugo—Abridged by James
K. Robinson—#R185—60¢

RODERICK RANDOM—by Tobias Smollett—#T158—75¢

THE SHORTER NOVELS OF HERMAN MELVILLE —introduction by Raymond Weaver—#D105—50¢

THE STORY OF AN AFRICAN FARM—by Olive Schreiner—
#D100—50¢

THAÏS—by Anatole France—#D126—50¢

TOM JONES—by Henry Fielding—Edited and abridged by
Somerset Maugham—#R174—60¢

TRISTRAM SHANDY—by Laurence Sterne—#T175—75¢

THE WAY OF ALL FLESH—Samuel Butler—#D94—50¢

WHEREVER PAPERBACK BOOKS ARE SOLD

If your dealer is sold out send only cover price plus 10¢ each for post-
age and wrapping to Premier Books, Fawcett Publications, Inc.,
Greenwich, Conn. If order is for five or more books, we pay postage.
No Canadian orders.

believe that she had all the virtues a woman can have without being a paragon that no one would put up with. I am well aware that I have not been able to show either in her or in any of the others what it was that made them the great writers they were. All but Tolstoy belonged to the middle class of society, and there is nothing that I have discovered in their ancestry or in their circumstances to account for their possession of a precious gift. Where the gift comes from, what it consists in, how it arises—all that, so far as I know, is inexplicable. It is a sport of nature. It seems to depend on the personality, and the personality seems compounded of estimable qualities and sinister defects. Having lived with these various people for so long, either through the medium of their books or through that of their biographies and letters, the conclusion has been forced upon me that they were on the whole not nice people. They may have been pleasant enough to meet, for, I repeat, with the exception of Emily Brontë whose shyness made her unsociable, they were good company. But they must have been hell to live with.

I will finish with a few scattered sentences from a book of Whitehead's which I happened to be re-reading while I was writing this piece. They seem to sum up pretty well all of the reflections I have had occasion to make in the course of this book.

"Human beings require something which absorbs them for a time, something out of the routine which they can stare at. Great art is more than a transient refreshment. It is something which adds to the soul's self-attainment. It justifies itself both by its immediate enjoyment, and also by its discipline of the inmost being. Its discipline is not distinct from enjoyment, but by reason of it. It transforms the soul into the permanent realization of values extending beyond its former self."

And finally, and this may be applied both to the authors of these books and to the books themselves:

"We must not expect, however, all the virtues. We should even be satisfied if there is something odd enough to be interesting."